EVANGELISM ENCOUNTER

D0879734

Brennan Bask

EVANGELISM ENCOUNTER

DICK SISSON

VICTOR BOOKS®
A DIVISION OF SCRIPTURE PRESS PUBLICATIONS INC.
USA CANADA ENGLAND

Unless otherwise noted, Scripture quotations are from *New American Standard Bible,* © the Lockman Foundation 1960, 1962, 1963, 1968, 1971, 1972, 1973, 1975, 1977. Bible quotations marked NIV are from the *Holy Bible, New International Version,* © 1973, 1978, 1984, International Bible Society. Used by permission of Zondervan Bible Publishers.

Recommended Dewey Decimal Classification: 248.5
Suggested Subject Heading: EVANGELISTIC WORK
Library of Congress Catalog Card Number: 87-62478
ISBN: 0-89693-445-4

© 1988 by SP Publications, Inc. All rights reserved. Printed in the United States of America. No part of this book may be used or reproduced in any manner whatsoever without written permission from the publisher, except in the case of brief excerpts in critical articles and reviews. For information address Victor Books, Wheaton, IL 60187.

CONTENTS

PART THREE
WHAT WILL IT TAKE? A METHOD!

PART FOUR
WHAT WILL IT TAKE? A MANIFESTATION!

To those I have known for their special gifts of evangelism: Ralph Merritt, Harry Saulnier, Lois Peterson, Lloyd Schumacher, Dan Fritz, Don Mersberger, Tom Frost, Diane Alme, Bob Hoel, Nick Repak, Jonathan Harris, Marty Klauber, and Micky Walker.

To George Verwer and the young evangelists of Operation Mobilization, especially to those ministering on the MV Logos and the MV Doulos.

And to the memory of Coach Dave McClain.

Acknowledgments

When a book is written over a period of fifteen years, it becomes the labor of many people. The author acknowledges his debt to Joan Morrick and Ruthanne Richmond for typing the early drafts of the manuscript. Special thanks to Dee McNamara for the final editing and typing, which required countless hours. Finally, I want to thank Gordon MacDonald, Gary Seaquist, Nate Mirza, Karen Gehrman, and my wife, Carol, for reading, revising, and making numerous suggestions for improving the text.

PREFACE

"It's a girl!" The words were familiar. Thousands of couples hear them every day. But this time, these three familiar words had an extraordinary ring. Dave and Debbie had been trying for six years to have a baby. They struggled valiantly—trying everything from special medications to painful surgeries—but to no avail.

After months of prayer, they felt led to begin adoption procedures. The process was agonizingly slow, but finally the word came. A beautiful little girl was available! She would be ready to take up residence with them in three weeks. Dave and Debbie were ecstatic! It may sound like a fairy tale, but the baby was delivered to their home on Christmas Eve—the gift of a lifetime, the gift of life.

Three months later, the grateful parents stood on our church platform to have their new daughter dedicated to the Lord. Dave is a scientist, a quiet man who doesn't wear his feelings on his sleeve. As I gave him the microphone to share a word of praise, however, I sensed that this was going to be a very special dedication service.

He tried to speak, but a lump in his throat made that impossible. The tears began to flow. Debbie squeezed his hand. The sanctuary was silent. Tears were streaming from nearly every eye. There was an unspoken understanding that this moment rightfully belonged to all of us. How many prayers had we uttered? How many words of encouragement? How many gifts had been given to prepare this family's nursery for this cherished newcomer?

Finally, Dave found the ability to share a few words. In essence he said, "We're grateful to God; we're grateful to you. You stood by us to make this moment possible. It is appropriate that we share our daughter and our joy with you."

What a lesson I learned that day! Becoming parents may involve a difficult and prolonged struggle, but it is always worth it. The struggle is so intense that couples can't "go it alone." The entire body of Christ is needed. Then, at last, the joy of birth explodes upon all.

The thesis of this book is that for evangelism—the birthing of spiritual babies—to be explosive in our age, the entire church family must be involved. There is a correlation between evangelism and worship, family life, corporate prayer, education, small-group dynamics, preaching, discipleship, and missions. We must sense that we are in this ministry together. But that's not all; the sharer of Christ must also sense that his or her own life is truly integrated with Christ. Our persuasiveness flows from our sincere belief that Christ has made a satisfying difference in our lives.

Evangelism is the product of harmony. There must be a synthesis between methodology and manner of life, between the believer and the "body," between what we learn in the classroom and what we learn on the streets.

To change the metaphor, music merely discussed satisfies no one, but when the concert begins—when instruments play in harmony—a very special kind of communication takes place. Evangelism is Good News about Christ communicated through the music of an authentic demonstration of the life of Christ. The whole church has a part to play. May we play in tune.

The world is waiting. Let the concert begin.

Dick Sisson

CHAPTER 1
What Will It Take?

But you shall receive power when the Holy Spirit has come upon you; and you shall be My witnesses both in Jerusalem, and in all Judea and Samaria, and even to the remotest part of the earth. (Acts 1:8)

Billy Graham's name has become almost synonymous with evangelism to many people. But when I think of evangelism, I think of a plumber I knew in Aurora, Nebraska—Ralph Merritt. I don't think I am exaggerating when I say that he left his mark on Hamilton County.

I was just twenty-five years old when my wife and I moved to Nebraska to start what would soon become the Aurora Evangelical Free Church. Ralph was well into his fifties when I stumbled across him (and thus I was quickly cured of the misconception that only young people are interested in evangelism). Not only was he twice my age, he was ten times as wise. Although he taught me much about following Christ, his greatest contribution to my thinking was in the area of evangelism.

One Man's Pattern
Ralph's idea of a good time was to grab a handful of Gospel tracts and tear down to the Hamilton County Jail. He would beam when he described his prison ministry. (There he sensed

that he had the unusual ability to hold his audience captive!) Many prisoners found new life in Christ.

Ralph lived his life with a conscious awareness that Christ was his Lord and that his life had a spiritual purpose. If there is one key to evangelism, it is this: *Successful soul-winners have a personal love affair with Christ.* To hear this simple country plumber share his faith was like listening to Romeo describe his romantic thoughts of Juliet. Ralph was really in love with Christ and it showed. Often he would cry when he spoke of Christ's sacrifice. When it came time to press for a decision for Christ, Ralph might squeeze a hand or grab a man's shoulders. This was not theatrics. People sensed his earnestness and responded. He led hundreds to Christ, almost always one at a time.

Because Ralph was in tune with God and because it was his daily prayer that God would lead him to a person searching for life's answers, I will always associate this verse with him: "Sanctify Christ as Lord in your hearts, always being ready to make a defense to every one who asks you to give an account for the hope that is in you, yet with gentleness and reverence" (1 Peter 3:15).

Certainly there were times when this daily act of personal consecration did not come easily to Ralph. He had his weaknesses and failings, but this old plumber did not live by feelings. He knew that life was a struggle. Sometimes, when he felt spiritually cold, he would withdraw to a quiet place and beg God to rekindle the flame for evangelism. God always honored this sincere request.

It wasn't long after Ralph won my heart that our Heavenly Father called him home. I will never forget how hard it was for the surrounding Christian community to imagine living without Ralph. In a curious kind of way, I don't face that problem, for Ralph is still with me. He profoundly influenced my thinking about evangelism.

One Man's Principles
When I reflect on Ralph's evangelistic success, I see that he consistently practiced workable biblical principles in talking to others about Christ. He is a worthy model of a layman who

found challenge and satisfaction in sharing his faith. I urge you to reflect on these principles.

Ralph involved the entire believing community in his ministry. This idea is no longer popular with those who believe that non-Christians should be spared the "culture shock" of meeting with God's people. Ralph never felt that way. He brought hundreds of visitors to our church. Even on the street, he made a point of introducing me to people as his pastor. Many times while sipping coffee at the local cafe, he would draw members of the Christian community into a spiritual discussion with one of his acquaintances. He often "volunteered" the services of a Christian tradesman who might help someone out (and also open a heart's door).

Ralph was convinced that only as people saw Christians in action would they feel drawn to Christ. This might be in the context of the family or the church or even through the way Christian friends responded to difficult situations. For instance, Ralph had a Christian coworker named Ron. Both were expert plumbers and consistently reflected a deep spiritual bond while working together. They were united in Christ's love and this spiritual reality always found a way to show itself to those outside the kingdom.

Ralph understood that evangelism was a process. He never felt compelled to force the issue. Time would open doors. Occasionally, in the context of developing a friendship, Ralph would ask pertinent questions about the meaning of life. Throughout this process, Ralph continued to engage the resources of the Christian community. He recognized weekly Bible studies as a valuable tool for winning people to Christ and allowing the Holy Spirit to accomplish His work.

Ralph was successful in establishing social contacts outside the evangelical community. He made it his business to get to know everyone and to "show himself friendly," and he was appreciated by young and old alike. I cannot help but feel that a contributing factor to the evangelistic failure of the twentieth-century church is that we have been neither creative nor sincere in developing and maintaining social contacts with unbelievers.

Since learning these specific insights and lessons from this dear man fifteen years ago, I have attempted to teach them in a classroom. Thus, for nearly ten years I have taught a workshop on personal evangelism every spring and fall. I am sure that Ralph would approve of the methodology used, but sometimes I feel as if he is tapping me on the shoulder and saying, "Dick, don't stress methodology. Stress the importance of knowing Christ, of being comfortable with people, of being sensitive to the Holy Spirit's timing." As I reflect on these thoughts, I ask, "What will it take to reach the world for Christ?" Rather than highlighting methodology for sharing the Gospel, I conclude that the need is to stress spiritual principles.

Evangelism isn't just broadcasting biblical data. Certainly we want to present solid biblical content; we want to help believers "pass their examinations" on the parts of the Gospel. People do graduate from our workshops having memorized three steps to this and four principles about that, but we do not produce Ralph Merritts in the classroom. Ralph's success was based on his determination to build his life around his commitment to Jesus Christ. Everything we do in our churches must have this as our goal, including evangelism training. Scriptural teaching about holiness, prayer, revival, body life, and knowing God cannot merely be assumed. It must be spelled out.

A Consistent Life

Evangelism is our attempt to share a personally fulfilling worldview with others. Our sharing is necessarily grounded in how we think and feel about the quality of our lives. We must be honest and sincere. This is the message of the eighties. Becky Pippert, in her wonderful book *Out of the Salt-Shaker* (Inter-Varsity Press), said:

> I used to worry constantly after witnessing to someone whether I did it right, if I should have said this or that, and so on. The Scripture calls us to excellence, but it also says the Spirit will give us what we need for tough situations (Mark 13:11). To be anxious about whether we have witnessed in exactly the "right way" implies there is some outside perfect standard that we are being judged by. But there is no magic

formula; there is no absolute and correct way to witness every time. We are called to do the very best we can, and then trust the Holy Spirit to speak to a person through what we say and do. (p. 129)

How wise she is. When Christ's love and mission consume us, evangelism can become a natural yet significant part of life. We can relax and be ourselves. Only such people are free to see, to feel, to help, to eliminate intimidating "God-talk." Becky asserts, "Few things turn off people faster or alienate them more easily than God-talk" (p. 130). She states:

We should talk the same way to non-Christians as we do to Christians. In most instances we should be able to tell both groups the same stories or experiences or thoughts. This will help us avoid having an us-and-them mentality. We should not assume that our non-Christian friends will not be interested in our spiritual side. We need to invite them into our lives, to share what we share, enjoy what we enjoy. We must not act superior because we know God or have more information. Rather, we must be, as someone has said, "one beggar sharing with another beggar where to find bread." (p. 130)

Joe Aldrich, in his book *Life-Style Evangelism* (Multnomah Press), suggests that one important result of having a spiritual focus is that through it we gain a greater appreciation of what others are feeling. The Holy Spirit gives us sensitivity. Aldrich urges us to get to know people so well that we have no difficulty relating our message to the point of felt need.

The whole Christian world is coming to the same conclusion. Evangelism is a way of life that is rooted in the lordship of Christ. It springs from the overflow of a heart consumed by God. Arthur McPhee reminds us that people are not stupid. They know who has the genuine article and who has "hot air." He says:

Both Christians and non-Christians are uptight about evange-lism. One reason why is because of the unnatural, canned approaches that are so often recommended and used. Christians want to share their faith, but not as high-pressure sales-men. Non-Christians, on the other hand, have grown wary of religious "zealots" who are out to corner them and put them on the spot. Who can blame either group? (preface, *Friend-ship Evangelism*, Zondervan)

Daily Dependence on God

Successful evangelism requires preparation. Certainly we must prepare our minds by considering strategy, methodology, and even a little theology. Some of our training can take place in a classroom, but not all of it. We must also prepare our hearts and learn how to overcome our fears. This kind of preparation can only take place on a spiritual battlefield. We can achieve victory only when we have wrestled with God in prayer and exchanged our weakness for His strength. Such warfare must be waged every morning. Waiting on God through contemplative prayer, reordering our priorities and schedules around His purposes, and enjoying His rejuvenating presence are what lead to spiritual revival.

My spiritual "temperature" is constantly changing. Sometimes, as my heart is revived in relation to my obedience, delight and urgency characterize my witness. At such times, sharing my faith is as natural as telling my friends how precious my wife, Carol, is to me. How natural evangelism (at least the desire to share) becomes when I am in rich, personal communion with the living Christ! Still, white-hot Christianity has a way of cooling off. Grad-ually, witnessing becomes a chore. When I neglect my soul, I lose perspective. God seems smaller. I get the feeling that people don't want to hear about Christ. I become defensive.

Consider the correlation between evangelistic energy and the ministry of the Holy Spirit in your life. Richard Owen Roberts has written a fascinating book, *Revival*. His thesis is that at cer-tain rare periods in the history of the church, God has visited this planet with spiritual revival. Such revivals have been nur-tured through prayer, repentance, and fasting. When the Spirit is poured out upon the world through such revival, an unparalleled evangelism explosion results. God alone, working through the Holy Spirit, is the source of fruitful evangelism.

Would you share your faith effectively? Get alone with God and give Him your life all over again. Deal with sins that rob you of spiritual single-mindedness. Make an end to every fleshly stumbling block and personal habit that stifles your zeal. Claim a new beginning. Ask God for the ability to appreciate important things. Wait upon Him for direction concerning personal priorities.

Fundamental to heart preparation is concentrated prayer. I think of two kinds of prayer. *Contemplative* prayer focuses on who God is, what He is doing, and how we fit into His purposes today. Such prayer is true worship. We pray in order to commune with the Lord God Almighty. As we pray, we remind ourselves of God's nature and attributes. We contemplate His will and slowly realign ourselves with His purposes. Read Psalm 143 for an example of such prayer. The theme is always "You are my God—I am Your servant!"

Through *intercessory* prayer, we actively petition God to open specific doors in evangelism. We beg Him to lead us into divinely arranged encounters through which we are able to share Christ, as the Apostle Paul did:

> With all prayer and petition at all times in the Spirit, and with this in view, be on the alert with all perseverance and petition for all the saints, and pray on my behalf, that utterance may be given to me in the opening of my mouth, to make known with boldness the mystery of the Gospel. (Eph. 6:18-19)

When we pray in this way, our entire day becomes a spiritual experience as we seek God's leading. Our faith grows as we experience God's faithfulness in providing us opportunities to share Christ with others.

A Prepared Mind

As hearts are prepared, we will develop a new appreciation for the unique importance of the Gospel. Warm hearts stimulate fertile minds. However, the twentieth-century church is really quite ignorant about the great historic systems of theology. These systems help us to relate all aspects of salvation to the complete spectrum of who God is and what He is doing. Should I believe in God's sovereignty in evangelism? What is the role of the Holy Spirit? What does the Bible mean by the word *repentance?* Few Christians have taken time to read a comprehensive systematic theology, such as that of Strong, Buswell, Hodge, Chafer, or Calvin. Not many have made a sincere attempt to sort through the issues of the new birth.

Saving truth should be handled as carefully as scientists handle plutonium. We would all profit from a serious exposure to a systematic theology of salvation. What divine purposes were realized through the cross? How can we understand what it scripturally means to "believe," and how can we account for the many different ways people define it? What does it mean to be "born again"? Is that just a figure of speech? Is the new birth a crisis (does it happen instantly) or a process (do we gradually experience it)? We must define terms and understand biblical facts before we pursue methods of sharing Christ with others.

A Vital Church

God intended the local church to be the legal evidence ("exhibit A") of the fact that He is mighty to save. But who is looking at the exhibit? In recent years we have been told that local churches consist of families of the faithful and non-Christians are not welcome in our assemblies. To understand what lies behind this notion, we must look at recent history.

As a World War II baby, I think I have lived through three epochs of evangelistic strategy in the local church. The first period extended from 1945 to the middle 1960s. During this epoch, the prevailing strategy centered on the evangelistic rally. The idea was to gather a crowd and preach the Gospel. The organization Youth for Christ used this approach with considerable success. Churches practiced a similar approach, with the pastor using his pulpit to evangelize. Altar calls followed sermons, and seekers were quietly whisked off to prayer rooms. Gradually, the rally died, losing its effectiveness because Christians did not encourage non-Christians to attend. Soon, only saints were being evangelized!

The second epoch began in the 1960s. Strategists began to

think, *If Mohammed won't go to the mountain, the mountain will go to Mohammed!* Through books like *Evangelism Explosion*, the church began to develop a strategy for evangelizing outside of the church. Joe Aldrich calls this method "confrontational-intrusional" evangelism because the sharer, though not invited, visits homes and seeks immediately to win a stranger to Christ. The sharer does not first cultivate a relationship, nor does he or she involve other Christians in the process. As a result sharing takes place apart from a convincing demonstration of why the message is relevant.

We are now entering a third epoch and turning an exciting corner. The local church is coming back into evangelism, but the pastor is no longer the primary evangelist! God's people are becoming aware that by encouraging friends to worship with them, they are beginning an evangelistic process. If churches function as they should, this brush with spiritual reality should prompt curiosity.

The time has come for God's people to work together in the exciting process of evangelism. I do not want to minimize the role of personal witnessing, but I do want to stress the potential of the visible church for offering a convincing demonstration of the life of Christ to the community. If you want to evangelize, be sure that you are attending a church that offers a genuine spiritual manifestation.

One pastor I know is persuaded that worship becomes visible when unity is evident in the midst of great diversity. The relevant ministry of the Word, spontaneous praise, caring service, and the application of moral principles interspersed with originality and creativity will serve to encourage others. You must be caught up with what God is doing in your church! If you are enthusiastic, inviting others to attend will be easy. You will then be confident that if visitors come, they will witness something quite extraordinary. They will see *God* at work. The fragrance of spiritual communion and worship will kindle a sense of wonder. But first they must see more than a social event. If your church offers no such convincing demonstration, don't be surprised if people are not more curious about the message of Christ. The church has a significant role to play in community penetration.

A Social Contact with the Community

If your church is like ours, programs may seem to start all over again each Labor Day. The wheels begin to spin in late summer. Leaders of every organization begin their frantic month of recruiting. Youth groups, music ministries, men's and women's organizations, and administrative and financial committees all solicit volunteers. Such recruitment programs are rather typical.

But I dream of entering the church foyer and seeing before me a huge poster that lists every civic and social organization that meets in our city. The list would include Boy Scouts, Rotary clubs, garden groups, and the Y.M.C.A. Can you imagine it? At the top of the poster would be these words: "Go ye into YOUR world and preach the Gospel!" The church would have a *penetration mentality*. Everyone in the fellowship would be encouraged to join a community organization. In doing so, the salt would come out of the saltshaker. We would have a whole new appreciation for what it means to be the salt of the earth.

During the past year, I began two community involvements that have influenced my thinking. First, I joined the Y.M.C.A. Though I originally joined for health reasons, I soon found that God had other purposes in view. I began to meet many other men and established a number of ongoing acquaintances. I have had more evangelistic opportunities and spiritual fruit from these associations than I have had in many years of confrontational witnessing. Many have visited our church and are in the process of putting their trust in Christ.

Second, I was elected to the governing body of the Walnut Grove Homeowner's Association. The Lord knew exactly what I needed. Attendance at these meetings has made me realize what tunnel vision I once possessed. Previously, I had virtually no contact with my neighbors or my community. Now, God is opening some wonderful doors! I am beginning to see the wisdom of McPhee's thesis as stated in the foreword by Myron Augsburger:

> The style of evangelism must be adapted to the times and the culture in which Christians are sharing faith. Friendship evangelism is one of the more universally acceptable methods

because it utilizes normal relationships. It has the potential of maximum participation of the membership of a congregation, and it offers a means of direct interchange with the public. And this sharing of faith is done in a context of loving acceptance of persons as individually important to us. (*Friendship Evangelism*, p. 11)

Take stock of your own situation. Apart from work, school, and church fellowship, who are your friends? Do you have any weekly contact within your community that offers you the opportunity of establishing a relaxed friendship through which you can gradually share Christ? Can you appreciate how your fears might dissolve if you didn't equate evangelism with unloading everything that you ever learned about the Gospel in one harried and forced conversation with a stranger?

If we really get serious about a penetration mentality, and if we are committed to evangelism as a long-term process, we may even conclude that it is not such a bad idea to allow community organizations to use our facilities. Such conclusions were unthinkable when the *fortress mentality* held sway several years ago. This mentality was characterized by the fear that exposure to anything secular or worldly might contaminate the church. The church was to maintain its purity by withdrawing completely from society. We were afraid that by allowing other groups to use our facilities, our testimony would be compromised.

Let me ask you to consider one more thought before we get into the nitty-gritty of evangelism training. I believe Ralph Merritt's love for sharing Christ was cultivated, not innate. He made decisions that enabled him to be more fruitful. There are decisions we must make if we are going to succeed in personal evangelism. Read on and let's make some of these decisions together.

Thinking It Over
- What does it take to produce evangelists like Ralph Merritt, the plumber? Do you think you can become like him?
- What evangelism principles can we learn from him?
- How can your church be a positive factor in your evangelism?

Do you feel comfortable inviting others to your services? Why or why not?

- What is meant by a "penetration mentality"?

PART ONE

What Will It Take?

A
Memory!

PROLOGUE TO PART ONE
UNDERSTANDING THE EVANGELISTIC DYNAMICS OF THE EARLY CHURCH

The four parts of this book approach the theme of evangelism from four different viewpoints: history, theology, methodology, and finally, philosophy. We could also say that we are trying to approach evangelism through the perspective of four important disciplines: biblical theology (Acts), systematic theology (the Gospel), practical theology (the plan), and pastoral theology (integrating evangelism into the life of the church).

When I get discouraged, I often turn to Acts, a truly gripping book, to get my spiritual batteries recharged. Can you imagine that these unlearned men and women succeeded in bringing the Gospel to all the world? In the following three chapters, we want to see how they shared their faith, overcame their fears, gained a hearing, stated their case, dealt with threats, and demonstrated their credibility.

In chapter 2 we emphasize the credibility of the early church. Before sharing a single word about Christ, these Christians demonstrated the life-changing power of the Holy Spirit who now indwelt them. We need to give some thought to the matter of our credibility. Why should anyone be interested in what we have to say? We had better have an answer for this question!

In chapter 3 we study the twin themes of Christianity that have triggered decisions for Christ for centuries—guilt, which states the problem, and grace, which offers a divine solution. The

Gospel, after all, is God's solution to a human problem we cannot solve by ourselves. In this light we realize that those who put their trust in Christ experience true deliverance. And this complete deliverance is God's gift, which we can receive without cost.

Finally, in chapter 4 we discuss practical insights about evangelism that grow out of our study in Acts. We'll pay particular attention to the various methods and processes of evangelism revealed in Acts and try to discover how these first Christians conquered their fears. Unless we help people today overcome their fear of sharing Christ, evangelism simply will not happen.

Luke opens Acts by stating that his first book, the Gospel of Luke, was the record of what Christ "began to do and teach" (Acts 1:1). Acts is the sequel, dealing with what Christ continues to do through the spiritual body we call His church. Acts has twenty-eight chapters—but the story is still going on. Let's be a part of it.

CHAPTER 2
The First Evangelism Explosion

And with a leap, he stood upright and began to walk; and he entered the temple with them, walking and leaping and praising God. And all the people saw him walking and praising God; and they were taking note of him as being the one who used to sit at the Beautiful Gate of the temple to beg alms, and they were filled with wonder and amazement at what had happened to him. (Acts 3:8-10)

Awesome! Everything is awesome! Do you know what I mean? A sportscaster describes a touchdown run by a star halfback as "awesome." My daughter comes home and describes the "totally awesome" pizza she just shared with a friend. No wonder words are losing their meanings!

We must admit that very few things are really awesome. What have you experienced lately that has taken your breath away with reverent and wondrous awe? Several years ago, a number of pastors were sitting around a lunch table at the Moody Pastors' Conference. Among them was Chuck Swindoll, who said, "Gentlemen, I don't know what's happening at our church. There's no human way to explain it. I think I preach as I did at my former church. One thing is certain. What we are experiencing is of God. I take no credit for it. In fact, I sometimes get a chill when I walk through the doors. God is working. I stand in complete awe of His saving power!"

In 1980 I had the opportunity to visit Paraguay with New Tribes Mission. It was my first exposure to both the jungle and the *chaco*, a vast desert lowland. God visited a tribe there in a most remarkable way. The Moro tribe was made up, literally, of headhunters. They stalked each other in a way that resembles the "naked savage" stereotype of the movies. Through the witness of faithful missionaries, a spiritual awakening began not too far from the German settlement of Filadelfia. Many of those who once found power in killing others now worship God. I am in awe of what God is doing there.

God of Wonder

Recently, I began a personal study of the Book of Acts. What happened in Jerusalem two thousand years ago gives new meaning to the word *awesome*. Unfortunately, Christians today tend to take it for granted. We must think it through all over again. As we consider these chapters, we must ask ourselves hard questions: Do I know this kind of God? This kind of salvation? This kind of urgency?

To capture the wonder of the days that followed the coming of the Spirit at Pentecost, a small dose of imagination will prove helpful. Iran has been in the news frequently. We are all familiar with the Ayatollah Khomeini. The militant fundamentalism he has brought to Iran stands in stark contrast both to the pleasure-centered worldview of the secular West and also to the spiritual principles of Christianity. Let's dream together about Iran. Can you imagine Pentecost coming to Tehran? Thousands of people turn to Christ. Bible studies spring up everywhere. Signs, wonders, and awesome demonstrations of the truth of Christianity are daily occurrences. This is precisely the kind of thing God brought about at Pentecost. He is awesome in power.

It is nevertheless difficult for many of us to think in such terms today. I am told that in the entire country of Saudi Arabia, there are no converted Moslems who could share their spiritual experience of coming to Christ with any fellow countryman and live. Societies of militant Moslems are bound by oath to report such "apostates." (In the Koran it is called the Law of Apostasy.) But we must not limit God. He hasn't lost His power. God is still awesome in strength and creativity.

We know with certainty what God can do because we are able to read His trustworthy account of what He has already done. The time is nearly two thousand years ago. One cannot visualize a more depressing scene for the disciples of Christ. The Messiah has just been crucified. His followers have lost heart. They feel powerless now that they are cut off from the source of so much of their inspiration. Then Christ appears to His followers in resurrection life. As He ascends into heaven, He promises that they will soon know His resurrection life in a personal and extraordinary way. He promises them the power of the Spirit. They return to Jerusalem to wait. All of a sudden the wind starts to blow....

We Need a Memory
As people in a secular age, we tend to forget what God can do, and such forgetfulness results in pessimism. This dullness of memory has brought about changes in the church's thinking about evangelism. When the church lacks an exalted view of God, its evangelism is reduced to dependence on high-gloss marketing techniques of human origin.

God is waiting for us to rediscover who He is. When we see Him as He is, we will want to serve Him and become His ministers of reconciliation. I pray that new doors for evangelism will spring open as we study and internalize God's Word, particularly the description in Acts of God at work in the Jerusalem church. What would happen if we started waiting on God in prayerful expectation? If we quietly sanctified Christ as Lord in our hearts? (1 Peter 3:15) If we reexamined our priorities? If we learned God's ways? If we again took the eternal destiny of people seriously? If we repented of our indifference and worldly preoccupations?

Two facts are clear. An evangelistic revolution took place in the first century, and now in the twentieth century we need another such revolution. Let's study Acts 1–3 as a unit. In chapter 1 we find the promises Christ made that ensure the church's success. In chapter 2 we discover the prerequisites for any significant evangelistic outreach. In chapter 3 these prerequisites are repeated in such a way as to suggest that a biblical pattern is forming.

The Promise of Evangelism

Pentecost, as recorded in Acts 2, marks the birth of the church, so what immediately precedes that historic event might be looked at as an incubation period for the still unformed church. Think of the physical birth process: For nine long months the embryonic child is taking form. Finally, at a moment in time the baby arrives. Study Acts 1 and you will see the church being prepared for its birth. Listen to Dr. Luke:

> The first account I composed, Theophilus, about all that Jesus began to do and teach, until the day when He was taken up, after He had by the Holy Spirit given orders to the apostles whom He had chosen. To these He also presented Himself alive, after His suffering, by many convincing proofs, appearing to them over a period of forty days, and speaking of the things concerning the kingdom of God. (Acts 1:1-3)

The author emphasizes that Jesus, even after His resurrection, had only begun His work. In one sense the work of redemption was finished when Christ gave His life at Calvary. But Christ would now work through a spiritual body, the church, to bring His truth and His fullness to the entire world. In Luke's introductory chapter, we read of three promises that Christ made to His yet unborn body that would guarantee its ultimate success.

The promise of a coming kingdom. Jesus Christ was not idle during those forty days between His resurrection and ascension. He taught purposely and persuasively about the kingdom of God. The Jews thought much about God's kingdom, but they must have been shocked by Christ's new teaching about the kingdom. The Saviour also promised the apostles that they would be "baptized with the Holy Spirit not many days from now" (v. 5).

When we combine the two ideas of the kingdom and the Spirit, we discover that God is establishing a kingdom by planting His Spirit in the inner lives of believers. Not only is the kingdom that future, millennial reign of Christ, but it is also a reality in the present tense. God's kingdom may be defined as "the sphere over which He rules." He reigns wherever Christ is Lord.

One day Christ will literally rule from the New Jerusalem. In this age, however, God does not rule through political entities, but His kingdom can still be made visible, as He displays His holy and powerful rule *through His church.* The mystery element of God's kingdom is a spiritual demonstration of love and righteousness through Christ's body (even when they live as a distinct minority in a Christ-rejecting culture).

How can people see God today? They see Him as the church reveals Him through their spiritual behavior, through truth lived out in relationships. *Evangelism cannot take place in an atmosphere that is void of a spiritual demonstration of the life of God.* Even before the church was born, Christ promised that the Holy Spirit would come and mold us into a spiritual organism so potentially awesome in unity and holiness that the world would acknowledge the uniqueness of Christ. Christ's reign over His kingdom would be evident in His church.

God's promise? In establishing His kingdom, God will give us the right *climate* for evangelism.

The promise of power. The second promise of Christ is given in response to a question. Again Luke writes:

And so when they had come together, they were asking Him, saying, "Lord, is it at this time You are restoring the kingdom to Israel?"

He said to them, "It is not for you to know times or epochs which the Father has fixed by His own authority; but you shall receive power when the Holy Spirit has come upon you; and you shall be My witnesses both in Jerusalem, and in all Judea and Samaria, and even to the remotest part of the earth." (vv. 6-8)

It was natural for Christ's disciples to read their own hope of the millennial kingdom into His words about a kingdom. They asked, "Is it time for Your kingdom to be established?" Christ's response to this question conveys an important lesson to us. It is not the *time* of Christ's reign but the *scope* of His kingdom that is important. Our calling is *to invite others to submit to His reign.* To put it differently, Christ laid a foundation for the church by mandating that His followers give themselves to the *expansion* of His kingdom. The Saviour is telling us that the truly significant task of this age is to enlarge Christ's mysterious kingdom, which we call the church.

For this important task, God has given us immense power. The secret of this age is the extraordinary power available to Christ's followers through the ministry of the Holy Spirit. How feeble our evangelistic strategies would be apart from the Holy Spirit!

What is God's promise? If we take seriously Christ's mandate to evangelize the world, God will give us sufficient *power* for evangelism.

The promise of the returning king. Christ spoke of a spiritual kingdom and a source of power that would be unleashed upon the earth. But there's more. We look now at the final promise:

> And after He had said these things, He was lifted up while they were looking on, and a cloud received Him out of their sight. And as they were gazing intently into the sky while He was departing, behold, two men in white clothing stood beside them; and they also said, "Men of Galilee, why do you stand looking into the sky? This Jesus, who has been taken up from you into heaven, will come in just the same way as you have watched Him go into heaven." (vv. 9-11)

All Christians are asked to live with eternity in their hearts. It has been well said, "We will have all of eternity to enjoy our crowns, but only a few brief moments of time to win them!" Christ is coming! He brings His rewards with Him. The church will always be pure and zealous when this truth is believed. The Lord Jesus, however, took careful pains to point out that His coming would be preceded by a long delay (see Matthew 25). Could the Pentecost momentum be sustained? Would Christ's followers gradually become earthbound?

Until Christ returns, we acknowledge that a primary reason for His delay is that His church is not yet complete. Peter tells us that we are to "regard the patience of our Lord to be salvation" (2 Peter 3:15). Every day that Christ delays His coming is a day in which more people have a chance to turn to Him in faith.

The promise of our Lord's return is not only an opportunity to evangelize; it is the constant hope through which we daily renew our spiritual vigor. Nothing is more effective in maintaining the Christian's zeal than the belief that Christ may return today.

I have never met you; yet, I am quite sure I can interpret your thinking. If you knew Christ was returning today, not only would you live purely, but you would spend much time on the phone telling everyone you love to prepare for His coming.

What is the meaning of this final promise? If we dare to live as if we believe Christ is coming soon, God will give us the *zeal* for evangelism.

The Prerequisites of Evangelism

Evangelism does not begin with an explanation. It begins with a *demonstration.* Paul urged the Romans to present their bodies as living and holy sacrifices, acceptable to God as a form of spiritual service (Rom. 12:1). He urged them to embrace a supernatural lifestyle that would be distinct from the worldly patterns of society. Why? So that we might *prove* that the will of God is good (Rom. 12:2).

One night I sat in a restaurant with a fifty-year-old man named Chet. He had given most of his life to the consumption of alcohol. With us was a friend of mine who used to be on the losing end of the battle with the bottle. Five weeks previous my friend Dave had put his trust in Christ, and Chet saw the difference. This is what he said: "I have known Dave for a long time. He always shares a smile, which I've come to associate with people who are trying to pretend that everything is fine. However, in the last few weeks, I've seen a change in Dave. He is not the same person I knew. He has a quiet confidence. Because of this change in Dave, I'm now convinced there might yet be hope for me!"

If this book has one overriding thesis, it is this: *Evangelism does not succeed because of a clever Gospel presentation. Our success will depend on a manifestation of spiritual reality in*

35

our lives. We learn these things from that memorable day called Pentecost. Consider the four components of the Pentecost evangelism explosion.

A convincing demonstration. Luke informs us, "When the day of Pentecost had come, they were all together in one place" (Acts 2:1). How perfect God's timing is! The Jewish Feast of Pentecost was a celebration of wheat harvest. If we studied passages like the twenty-third chapter of Leviticus, we would see that the Old Testament Feast of Pentecost was God's way of preparing His people for the harvest to come. Just so, Pentecost prepared the early church for the spiritual harvest we now realize is the evangelization of the world. In the Jewish calendar, there is a logical sequence of feasts. First comes the Passover, which symbolizes to us Christ's crucifixion. Then comes the Feast of First Fruits, which symbolizes to us Christ's resurrection. Next comes the Feast of Pentecost, which symbolizes to us the "harvest" of souls of those who would put their trust in the risen Christ.

Christ's followers were all together in an upper room in Jerusalem. Perhaps they were reflecting on the Old Testament meaning of Pentecost. Could it be that on that occasion Peter said to Matthew, "Matt, there's something special about today. Long ago our fathers used this day to celebrate the prospect of a bountiful harvest. What kind of harvest do you think God wants us to celebrate today?"

It happened suddenly. First, the people of Jerusalem were frightened by a great noise that sounded like a hurricane. Everyone heard it. This violent, rushing wind symbolized the power of the Holy Spirit.

Next "tongues as of fire" rested upon the heads of the apostles. Did these fiery tongues dance on the heads of the early saints? Did these heaven-sent flames flicker out of the mouths of Christ's first witnesses? Ray Stedman suggests that these fiery tongues symbolized the passionate, purifying preaching of the Gospel that would bring Christianity to the ends of the known world within a generation.

Finally, we learn that "they were all filled with the Holy Spirit and began to speak with other tongues, as the Spirit was giving them utterance" (v. 4). By a sovereign act of God, these un-schooled men were able to speak eloquently in languages previously unknown to them. This miraculous enablement declared the greatness of God.

My purpose in writing about Pentecost is not to raise questions about the charismatic controversy. I simply want you to recognize that the first great evangelistic adventure in the church was a direct result of a supernatural demonstration of the power of God.

Where is this demonstration today? Consider for a moment how many radio and television broadcasts now beam the Gospel over the airwaves. Consider how many boxes of Gospel literature are circulated every day. Think also of the thousands of conversations God's people have with non-Christians. Nevertheless, there is little fruit. Could it be that both worldliness in the church and thoughtless traditionalism have conspired to rob us of a convicting demonstration?

A curious fascination. This divine demonstration accomplished God's purpose. Those who witnessed these phenomena were stunned. Luke tells us that Jerusalem's citizens "were amazed and marveled" (v. 7). He also says that they continued in amazement and great perplexity, saying to one another, "What does this mean?" (v. 12)

God had these confused people right where He wanted them. For years, life had droned on in a business-as-usual fashion. The politically enslaved people of Jerusalem accepted the depressing conclusion that there was no hope on their horizon. A pervasive sense of futility robbed them of all creative aspiration, but now they were seeing the hand of God. They were amazed! God had succeeded in getting their attention.

Do you remember when Christ preached to a crowd in a little cottage? Suddenly, the roof tiles were shaken loose and a group of concerned men lowered a paralytic through the roof with the hope that he might be healed by Christ. Mark records the story in Mark 2:1-12. Christ told the man that his sins were forgiven him. The scribes who were present shouted, "Blasphemy!" The Saviour told them they would not believe His words until they saw a demonstration. " 'In order that you may know that the Son of Man has authority on earth to forgive sins,' He said to the paralytic, 'I say to you, rise, take up your pallet and go home'" (vv. 10-11). Mark records that this was done "in the sight of all; so that they were all amazed" (v. 12). The last thing we hear from the lips of this awestruck mob are these telling words: "We have never seen anything like this" (v. 12).

Some of you are thinking, "But wasn't Pentecost a one-time event? Didn't God accompany the birth of the church with special signs and wonders? God is not doing these things in the twentieth century, is He?" I am enough of a supernaturalist to affirm that God is still giving His church authority and power to produce a continuous demonstration before an unbelieving world. One aspect of this demonstration can be recognized where saints are assembled—local churches, Christian homes, campus Christian groups, etc. "These people really love each other!" (See John 13:35.) Just as people can sense friction in relationships, they can see that Christians have a spiritual bond between them.

John wrote concerning Christ, "In Him was life; and the life was the light of men" (John 1:4). Sometimes very profound truths are hidden in very familiar verses. I think John is saying that the life of Christ is so extraordinary that it stands out like a beacon. What is it that sets some Christians apart and makes the world take note of them? They quietly display the spiritual life of Christ, and this life makes them shine. It leads others to the conclusion, "I think this person has his life together."

Are you satisfied that there is a demonstration of the mysterious life of Christ in the local church you attend? Every witnessing Christian ought to attend a church that is marked by authentic spiritual reality. We feel excitement about bringing non-Christians into this kind of atmosphere. We do not expose our friends to spiritual worship to "get them converted" but to instill in them a sense of wonder.

A credible explanation. Note well that Peter's Pentecost sermon was really an answer to a question. The people asked, "What's going on here?" Peter responded, "I'm glad you asked. Here's the scoop." Peter told everyone that this unique manifestation was God's way of confirming that He was satisfied with

Christ's atoning work on the cross and that Jesus Christ was now exalted at the right hand of God the Father. Peter concluded his sermon by saying, "Let all the house of Israel know for certain that God has made Him both Lord and Christ—this Jesus whom you crucified" (Acts 2:36). While Peter was sharing the saving message of Christ, the Holy Spirit was doing His convicting work. The shaken crowd responded by inquiring, "What shall we do?" (v. 37)

Peter told them to repent, which means to turn to God's way of saving people from their sins. They were to look to Jesus Christ alone as their hope of eternal life and after placing their trust in Jesus as Saviour, they were exhorted to announce this new relationship through the ordinance of water baptism.

A conversion explosion. I began this chapter by saying that there are few things in life that are truly awesome, but the result of Peter's Pentecost sermon was surely one of them. Three thousand people turned to Christ. Don't forget that many of these people were probably present when the multitude screamed "crucify Him" just seven weeks before (Luke 23:21). I frankly confess that it is not easy for me to come to terms with the wonder of Pentecost. God poured out His Spirit upon Jerusalem and an evangelism explosion took place that is still rocking the world. Three thousand people not only said yes to Christ in their hearts but also took a public stand through baptism. Every pool in Jerusalem was being occupied that day!

The Pattern of Evangelism
I remember the first sermon I preached on Acts 3, many years ago. My thesis was that Peter's Pentecost sermon was so revolutionary that it demanded some kind of authentication. How could Peter persuade his listeners that Jesus Christ truly rose from the dead and was now ascended, glorified, invincible, and worthy of worship? He authenticated his message through a sign miracle. He healed a helpless cripple. I argued that chapters two and three should be seen as an unbroken continuum: a resurrection sermon is confirmed as Peter commands an invalid to walk in the name of Jesus.

There might, however, be a better way to relate these two

chapters. Is it possible that the same four-part evangelism cycle we just studied in Acts 2 (demonstration, fascination, explanation, explosion) is repeated all over again? Peter heals, the crowd wonders, Peter explains, and thousands are converted. The situation has changed, but the evangelistic process is essentially the same. Could it be that a pattern is developing?

A First-Century Miracle

Let's follow Peter and John as they walk into the courtyard at the temple area. It is three o'clock in the afternoon, time for prayer. People are scurrying in every direction, and it's kind of a "business as usual" scene. Predictable cosmopolitan sounds almost drown out the mournful wails of a beggar crying out for alms.

Peter and John pass within a few feet of this unfortunate man. Peter is apparently moved by the sight of this helpless man, for he says, "Look at us." The beggar's eyes gain intensity. Experience has conditioned him to anticipate that a small coin is about to be thrown his way, but Peter has a greater treasure in mind. "I do not possess silver and gold, but what I do have I give to you: In the name of Jesus Christ the Nazarene—walk!" (v. 6)

It is Peter who takes the initiative. He walks to the cripple, extends his arm, and pulls the man to his feet. Immediately, new strength comes to the crippled man's legs. In fact, he suddenly begins to walk and leap. He tearfully cries out to the God whose name is Jehovah and shouts his gratitude.

Luke records that the whole city watched him walk and leap off the ground and praise God (v. 9). He writes, "They were taking note of him as being the one who used to sit at the Beautiful Gate of the temple to beg alms, and they were filled with wonder and amazement at what had happened to him" (v. 10). The word spread like shock waves. A crowd gathered quickly. All of those who assembled had one thing in common. They were all "full of amazement" (v. 11). God's convincing demonstration had accomplished its purpose.

Demonstration gave way to fascination. It always does. People have continually been more fascinated by what others do than by what they say. Don't be surprised. You would be similarly "filled with wonder" if your crippled father suddenly leapt out of bed and took a jog around town!

As before, fascination prompted explanation. As you study Peter's second sermon, you will discover that his Gospel message is the same, but his emphasis is a little different. He stresses the guilt of his countrymen in their recent passion to see Christ crucified. Then, suddenly, he extends an invitation to his listeners to avail themselves of God's grace. These twin themes of guilt and grace are very important. I call them the "triggers of the heart" because they move people to repentance.

Peter's preaching evoked a heated response from his listeners. Few could remain neutral. The authorities, hardened by years of religious hypocrisy, were so outraged that they quickly hustled Peter off to the nearest prison cell.

But there was also another reaction. Thousands of those who listened were broken by the Spirit. With repentant hearts, they put their trust in Peter's Messiah (Acts 4:4). Bible scholars tell us that the escalating numbers of the infant Jerusalem church may now have approached 15,000 people. The explosion goes on!

Twentieth-Century Miracles?

If successful evangelism is rooted in a convincing demonstration, and if such a demonstration requires an undeniable display of the power of God, we must face these questions: Do miracles still happen? Do our churches still bear evidence of the supernatural? How will God's sovereign power manifest itself today?

I do not know of an evangelical pastor in America today who doesn't hunger for an outpouring of God's Spirit on his community. So many of my colleagues in the ministry have made unsatisfying attempts to teach evangelism classes in their churches. Together we must confess our disappointment that the kind of evangelistic explosion we hoped to inspire has failed to materialize.

Still, God has been patient with me. Several summers ago I had the privilege of spending a month off the coast of Finland aboard Operation Mobilization's ministry ship, the MV *Logos*. My whole family remarked afterward that when we boarded the vessel, we opened ourselves to an experience like that of first-century Christians.

Young people from twenty-five countries made up the ship's crew. They displayed a harmony and mutual concern such as I have rarely seen. Earnest prayer was offered continuously for God to pour out His Spirit in every port soon to be visited. I have never seen such zeal and enthusiasm in bringing the claims of Christ to people everywhere. They took to the streets, canvassed the bus terminals, and invaded the marketplaces. It wasn't long before they won the hearts of many of the curious Finns. The miracle of conversion occurred over and over and over.

Miracles are still happening, but never by accident and seldom in the way we expect! I fear we are so consumed by the sensational that we forget God's profoundly quiet miracles—conversion, joy in the midst of pain, self-sacrifice, entrenched patterns of sin overcome by the power of God, Christians who differ bound together by a deeper love.

One quiet miracle, oft repeated, is the concern God gives His people for their neighbors. Recently a friend of mine, a Christian medical student, took three hours out of studying for his medical exams to help a Taiwanese couple put together their Ping-Pong table. It is this kind of miracle, this kind of demonstration of the life of Christ that does more to prepare hearts for the kingdom than anything I know.

When will we open our spiritual eyes and admit that apart from such miracles our evangelistic efforts are not likely to bear fruit? God is waiting for His church to realize they need Him! How patient He is with us. He wants to do a great work through us. The quiet miracles begin when saints seek His face. Books on evangelism theory do not guarantee miracles. The missing link in contemporary evangelism is that fresh display of the true life of Christ in us.

I am now committed to the proposition that if we were living as God intended His people to live, we could bring disheartened, cynical people to our homes and worship services and ignite such a spark of hope within them that they would determine to know this Saviour of ours. No wonder God's people in so many communities are banding together to pray for revival. Only when God meets and blesses His people, only when the quiet miracles begin, will the world take note.

Don't Miss the Pattern of Pentecost

We learn an invaluable lesson about true evangelism by thinking through the sequence of the events of Pentecost. It all began with a *demonstration* of the power of God that could not be ignored. God was mightily at work here. His activity in the lives of His people could be seen and heard and felt. The predictable response of the crowd was *fascination*. Men and women were filled with amazement and wonder. "We have never seen anything like this before! What does it mean?" Fascination precipitated a logical *explanation*. This is the right environment for spiritual sharing. Peter held his audience captive as he delivered his first sermon about the saving power of Jesus Christ. This explanation triggered an *explosion*. Three thousand converts became the instant nucleus of this infant movement. Word spread quickly throughout the Roman world. The church age had begun. Nothing could stop it. God was at work. Nothing would be the same again.

Thinking It Over

- What were the three promises given by the Lord in Acts 1? How do they contribute to our understanding of evangelism?
- What was the fourfold sequence of evangelism revealed on the Day of Pentecost?
- Why is it necessary that people see in Christians a demonstration that creates amazement?
- Why aren't more non-Christians fascinated by the faith of Christians today?
- How does the healing in Acts 3 confirm the evangelism pattern of Acts 2?

CHAPTER 3
The Saving Chemistry of Guilt and Grace

And the Law came in that the transgression might increase; but where sin increased, grace abounded all the more. (Romans 5:20)

Many define religion as "the fine art of emotional manipulation." The converted are life's suckers; conversion is by coercion. Members of an organization called Fundamentalists Anonymous argue that people stay religious only through mind games. I think these people have a message that God's people need to hear. We need to be delivered from the mistaken idea that by mastering techniques we can ensure conversions.

What then, does trigger the mysterious decision-making process in the human heart? What prompts the inner man to respond to God? Can we discover in the Book of Acts spiritual secrets that tell how the Holy Spirit uses the witness of a Christian to bring about conversion? Just how is an individual moved, convicted, and broken by the Spirit? Why do some respond to God while others scoff?

The psalmist reminds us, "Salvation belongs to the Lord" (Ps. 3:8). Paul cautioned us against trying to understand spiritual mysteries known only to God. "How unsearchable are His judgments and unfathomable His ways! For who has known the mind of the Lord?" (Rom. 11:33-34) Recognizing our finiteness and our limitations, we ought to search the Scriptures for clues to how people are spiritually prepared to turn to Christ.

The evangelism explosion described in Acts supplies relevant data about this issue. People responded dramatically to Peter's preaching as he wove into his sermons the great interplay between two important Christian concepts: human guilt and divine grace. When people experience true guilt, they ask the question, What can I do? When they understand God's grace, they come to Christ wholeheartedly. Open-minded people don't need pressure; they need truth about their need and God's amazing provision. These truths do indeed trigger a sincere heart response. They work in our culture as they did in Peter's.

In the last chapter we described the amazement that resulted when a crippled man suddenly began walking and leaping and praising God (Acts 3). Demonstration gave way to fascination. Now it was time for explanation. Note how naturally Peter got through to the hearts of the people in the sermon that followed. Look at how powerfully God used Peter's emphases on human guilt and divine grace.

Peter begins, "Men of Israel, why do you marvel at this, or why do you gaze at us, as if by our own power or piety we had made him walk?" (Acts 3:12) Jesus Christ was responsible for this miracle. This was a clear demonstration of His resurrection power.

Peter's Word of Guilt

Having channeled the attention of this mob to the person of Christ, Peter presents a convincing case that the people of Israel shamefully brutalized this Nazarene without a just cause. Peter makes skillful use of contrast to heighten his listeners' growing sense of personal guilt.

Peter's sermon in Acts 3:12-26 relates five specific contrasts between who Christ really is and the shameful way the people of Jerusalem treated Him. First, Jesus Christ came to earth as the *servant Messiah*—the fulfillment of the covenant promise that through Abraham's seed God's blessing would come upon the entire world. But instead of looking at Jesus as the fulfillment of the servant-Messiah prophecies of the Old Testament, this same

45

crowd shouted, "Crucify Him!" Peter told them, "You delivered up" your Deliverer! (v. 13)

Second, God the Father has now glorified the Son. Christ now enjoys the center stage of heaven! But this mob disowned Him as a citizen of Israel and shamefully placed His destiny into the hands of a cruel Gentile named Pontius Pilate (Acts 3:13).

Third, Peter contrasts the character of Christ with the character of the man the Jews asked to be released in His stead. Christ is "the Holy and Righteous One" (v. 14). The Saviour not only displayed conduct that was above reproach, but also His inner being was pure and His mind was entirely free from the perversity that has so obviously tainted the minds of sinful men and women. But when the people were given the choice between freeing Jesus and freeing the notorious murderer Barabbas, they chose the latter (Acts 3:14).

Fourth, Peter calls Christ "the Prince of life." He had heard the Master say that He was "the resurrection and the life" (John 11:25). He understood that this was Christ's way of affirming His deity. Christ had said, "Just as the Father raises the dead and gives them life, even so the Son also gives life to whom He wishes" (John 5:21). Peter tells his Jerusalem listeners that, ironically, they "put to death the Prince of life" (Acts 3:15).

Finally, Peter addresses the attitude of the people to the healing wonder that had just been performed. Peter insists, "It is the name of Jesus which has strengthened this man whom you see and know; and the faith which comes through Him has given him this perfect health in the presence of you all" (Acts 3:16). In his final word of contrast, Peter tells his now convicted listeners that instead of giving Christ credit for this healing, they were content to chalk it up to the skill of two of Christ's followers.

Peter believed people had to face their guilt. Without such an awareness, there would be no heart cry for spiritual deliverance. Peter understood what twentieth-century evangelists must understand: *Salvation means deliverance from sin and its consequences.* Peter was not willing to do what some of us find so easy to do—ignore the reality of personal guilt. He knew that until individuals face their guilt, they will sense no need of a Saviour.

In our day we almost blush to bring up the subject of sin. We feel much more comfortable when we tell others that Jesus is our friend and He can be their friend too. We are not very comfortable with words like *repentance.*

Evangelism is risky business. It takes courage to tell people the truth about their spiritual condition. The same message that brings conviction to some brings outrage to others. Paul calculated the risk and concluded that the potential for new life in Christ justified the danger. He was able to conclude, "I rejoice in my sufferings for your sake" (Col. 1:24).

In the same way, Peter took risks when he preached the Gospel. It appears that he went out of his way to describe the guilt of his listeners in Acts 3. His courage stemmed from his belief that the Gospel of grace (divine provision for helpless sinners) is compelling only to people who have a sense of their own sinfulness.

Peter's Word of Grace

If Peter shows courage, he also shows sensitivity. Harsh words are offered as a necessary medicine, but he is not primarily concerned with finger pointing. He is merely stripping away comfortable rationalizations which might blind some to their need of Christ.

Peter apparently sees that his words have taken hold. Suddenly, his tone changes. His words take on a conciliatory tone as he suggests that this temple throng acted in ignorance when they screamed for Christ's crucifixion.

Had Peter stopped here, his offer of grace would have been nothing but hollow pity. The fact of ignorance was no longer acceptable. They had seen the Christ crucified! They had heard the accounts of those who had encountered the risen Christ. They could no longer be passive about His identity.

As the crowd listened to Peter, all the pieces started fitting together. How obvious it now was that scores of messianic prophecies were fulfilled by Christ. The prophets, beginning with Samuel, spoke of a servant Messiah who would suffer for His people and warned that disaster awaited those who turned a deaf ear to this Messiah. "Every soul that does not heed that prophet shall be utterly destroyed" (Acts 3:23).

Peter extends a gracious invitation. God has raised up His Son to bless them! He gave His life at Calvary "to bless you by turning every one of you from your wicked ways" (Acts 3:26). As Peter's hearers turned to Christ in faith, they would experience "times of refreshing . . . from the presence of the Lord" (Acts 3:19). If guilt underscores the problem, grace announces God's solution! Guilt reminds us of the sin burden we carry; grace lifts that burden. Guilt yields repentance; grace leads to regeneration. Together, they are God's triggers of the heart—the principal elements of God's saving chemistry.

Guilt in the Twentieth Century

People have never eagerly embraced a spiritual message that reminds them of their sin and guilt. The Apostle Paul told his Roman readers that when human conscience is stirred, predictable face-saving psychological responses are quietly activated (Rom. 2:15). When their consciences are pricked, people will either blame the problem on someone else (accuse) or rationalize it away (excuse).

Psychological rationalizations of true moral guilt have become something of an art form in our day. Pop psychologists encourage such rationalizations. This sad fact is pointed out in William K. Kilpatrick's unsettling book *Psychological Seduction* (Thomas Nelson). Everyone seeking to communicate spiritual truth should read this book, which can help us grasp the immensity of the challenge of sharing Christ with modern men and women.

Kilpatrick maintains that current psychological thought rests on three disturbing propositions. First, *self-esteem has become life's highest goal.* Absolutely nothing is more important than feeling good about yourself. He says, "This business of liking oneself has become for us almost a first principle" (p. 36). Every Christian knows there is a proper place in God's scheme of things for healthy self-acceptance, but the current view leaves God (and His image within us) out of the picture completely. Modern psychologists are now saying things like "Self-love means accepting yourself as a worthy person because you choose to do so" or "You are worthy because you say it is so."

Kilpatrick believes that much of the self-help literature of our age is designed to help people create their own self-esteem by the power of suggestion. It is like saying, "I am the most brilliant person in the world because I say I am."

Such thinking leads to a second popular proposition: *It is easier to change one's beliefs than it is to change one's behavior.* If we are truly persuaded that self-esteem is life's highest goal (and that nothing is more important than feeling good about ourselves), we will discover that our belief structure has become expendable. In this regard, Kilpatrick says, "It is possible to create a climate in which people have very little sense of sin and, therefore, little chance of comprehending what Christianity is all about" (p. 74). Why? Because psychology has been so enormously successful in helping people redefine into acceptable terms the patterns of behavior they cannot change.

Psychology has revolutionized the way people view guilt. Kilpatrick says, "Even when they feel guilty, they are convinced it is only neurotic guilt: not a matter for expiation but for explanation" (p. 74). In other words, the guilty are finding some comfort in the popular words of their therapists: "Your problem is not sin but sickness!"

Kilpatrick summarizes this thinking: "If our actions aren't in line with our beliefs, then we ought to change the beliefs (beliefs being considerably easier to change than behavior)." He then gives this example: "If your self-concept won't let you feel good about having casual sex, and yet you still want casual sex, then you ought to adjust your self-concept accordingly. The alternative is feeling bad about yourself, and that seems an almost unacceptable alternative these days" (p. 75).

The third pillar of pop psychology insists that *one's mental attitude is life's ultimate reality.* If people are encouraged to change beliefs in order to feel good, is it any wonder such people see reality in completely personal and subjective terms?

At one time, people thought in objective terms about an objective universe. The Apostle Paul could tell people, "Christ is risen," and his hearers might have said, "No, that's not possible. Resurrections are simply not possible." The thoroughly modern man would probably respond quite differently to Paul's message:

"Hey, that's OK for you, but I'm into channeling. Whatever turns you on."

People do not argue about philosophical issues anymore. There is no longer an objective universe to argue about (so they say). Psychologists now tell us that we make our own reality. We can do anything we believe we can do. Success is a matter of believing hard enough. Kilpatrick says, "Our society is already more than half-convinced that subjective realities are superior to objective ones. Notice the constant chatter about arriving at your own truths or not imposing your values on others, as though truth and value were purely personal constructs and had nothing to do with things outside yourself" (p. 50). He concludes, "We tend to evaluate beliefs by their degree of personal meaning rather than by an objective criterion.... The current wisdom has it that truth is something that makes you feel good" (pp. 50-51).

The Importance of Facing Guilt

The Bible asks us to face our guilt rather than simply redefine it. When we do face our guilt, we crave a spiritual resolution. That is, we seek a way of coming into harmony with the holy God at the center of all things.

A person must turn to Christ for a better reason than that he is emotionally down. Peter, Paul, and all of the first-century evangelists shook people to the core by emphasizing that we live in a real world and are personally accountable to a real God for real sins committed in real life. Should we ignore the claims of Christ, we will continue to reap the real consequences of spiritual bondage.

Only when we grasp how secular our society has become will we appreciate how difficult the task of the modern evangelist is. We must not only win a hearing, but we must also offer an explanation of reality that is grounded in givens that are no longer widely accepted. That a person may scoff at the notion of resurrection does not make Christ's resurrection untrue. That people say they have no conscience problems resulting from immorality doesn't mean they are any less guilty.

Unless people are confronted with real guilt, real sin, and real consequences of their sinful behavior, they will never understand why they need a Saviour. The biblical picture of salvation corresponds to the idea of *deliverance* (Heb. 2:15). Until we know what binds us, we will sense no need of a deliverer. Likewise, the awareness of disease must precede the appropriation of a cure.

The realization of true moral guilt has been a turning point throughout biblical history. The Lord's response to Adam's original disobedience was to ask, "Where are you?" (Gen. 3:9) He asked Adam and Eve—the first fallen couple—to take careful stock of their new predicament. Joseph's brothers, after being put in prison, realized they were reaping what they had sown long before, when they had betrayed their brother and sold him into slavery. Through their own harsh confinement they came to their senses. "Surely we are being punished because of our brother. We saw how distressed he was when he pleaded with us for his life, but we would not listen; that's why this distress has come upon us" (Gen. 42:21, NIV). They concluded sadly, "Now we must give an accounting for his blood" (42:22).

Has it occurred to you how little true guilt is experienced today? Pop psychology has explained it all away. When people sense no guilt, they feel no need to turn to Christ. Listen again to William Kilpatrick:

> Christianity doesn't make sense without sin. If we are not sinners, turned away from God, then there is no reason for God to become a man, and no reason for Him to die. Our slavery to sin is the thing that Christ came to free us from. That is the most fundamental Christian belief. It follows that if you have no consciousness of sin, you simply won't be able to see the point of Christianity. We can put the matter more strongly and say that once you grant the notion that people are sinless, you must admit that Christianity is all wrong. (p. 74)

It is time to reintroduce our society to biblical reality. Let our message stress that Christ offers a true solution to the real problem of sin and guilt. A society determined to feel good about itself may feel uncomfortable with the questions we ask, but it is important that these questions be asked. Are people who rebel against God in true danger? Can our sins actually cut us off from His presence forever? Do heaven and hell disappear simply because we ignore them? If we are truly sinful, what hope is there for experiencing peace with God?

As people face these questions, they ought to be sobered, some even broken. Then guilt will have accomplished its purpose. This will not happen until our human rationalizations and defense mechanisms are abandoned. Because human beings are face-saving creatures, the task of the modern evangelist is not easy.

Grace in the Twentieth Century

Divine grace is the biblical counterpoint to human guilt. When sinful men and women grasp their lostness and wonder if there is any hope, they are ready to discover the good news that there is hope in Christ. In the New Testament, God's grace is always seen in connection with the ministry of Jesus Christ. John declares Christ to be "full of grace and truth" (John 1:14). Paul said, "For you know the grace of our Lord Jesus Christ, that though He was rich, yet for your sake He became poor, that you through His poverty might become rich" (2 Cor. 8:9).

But what do we mean by grace? Grace is God's way of providing the righteous standing that we lack and removing the guilt of our sinfulness through our faith in Christ. In other words, Christianity is good news about a great exchange.

The infinitely wealthy Son of God looks at sinfully bankrupt humanity and says, "I will exchange what I have for what you have! Give Me your sin and I will give you My righteousness. Let Me exchange My wealth for your poverty." This is just what happened at the cross. The Bible says God "made Him who knew no sin to be sin on our behalf, that we might become the righteousness of God in Him" (2 Cor. 5:21).

One would imagine that needy people would accept gladly this message of grace. But for grace to be attractive, people must finally realize that they have nowhere else to turn. Grace is beautiful only to the guilty. When the innocent go to court to present their case, they fight for justice. When the guilty enter the same room, they can only seek the mercy of the court. Spurgeon declared:

> What an abyss is the grace of God! Who can measure its breadth? Who can fathom its depth? Like all the rest of the divine attributes, it is infinite. God is full of love, for "God is love." God is full of goodness; the very name "God" is short for "good." Unbounded goodness and love enter into the very essence of the Godhead. It is because "His mercy endureth forever" that men are not destroyed; "His compassions fail not" that sinners are brought to Him and forgiven. (*All of Grace*, p. 41)

Guilt and grace should be seen as a couplet, for one can only be appreciated with the other. Guilt truly comprehended is devastating. But it opens us to seek God's grace. Guilt leads us to repentance; grace leads us to place our faith in Christ alone as our hope. Guilt is the awareness of what we are apart from Jesus Christ; grace declares that we have a new identity through Jesus Christ. Guilt brings us down; grace lifts us up. Guilt pricks our consciences to conclude that we cannot do enough to save ourselves. Grace produces a sense of wonder as we realize that we were saved for Christ's sake. Paul captured this sense of wonder when he wrote,

> For while we were still helpless, at the right time Christ died for the ungodly.... God demonstrates His own love toward us, in that while we were yet sinners, Christ died for us. (Rom. 5:6, 8)

Misconceptions about Grace

The biblical doctrine of grace is so otherworldly, so unlike human thinking, that it should not come as a surprise that it has been misunderstood throughout the centuries. Let me share with you three ways in which the subject of God's grace is obscured.

Grace is confused with sacrament. During the Middle Ages,

certain views came into the church that virtually transformed it from a company of redeemed men and women into a "salvation station" through which weekly installments of salvation could be obtained. During this time, it was commonly believed that the church was like a big ship steaming toward heaven. People thought if they could climb on board the institutional church, they would be safe. In other words, the focus of faith changed from "Christ crucified" to the church and its sacraments, which had to be administered by a priest.

With this change in the church came a dramatic alteration of the meaning of grace. Now, it seemed, God's favor was available to sinful people through the sacraments. As churchgoers partook of the sacraments, "grace" was made available to them in the form of imparted righteousness. This "grace" enabled people to become righteous enough for God to finally accept them. Such ideas are foreign to the Bible.

Grace is confused with selfishness. Have you ever heard a young Christian say, "I am saved by God's grace and I can do anything I want"? This well-meaning young believer is trying to emphasize that we are not saved through personal performance or self-reformation, which is true. But grace is never an inducement to selfishness. "For you were called to freedom, brethren; only do not turn your freedom into an opportunity for the flesh, but through love serve one another" (Gal. 5:13). Grace provides a way out of the self-dominated life. When we say, "I can do anything I want," we are not defining grace, but sin. Sin is the determination to live independently of God and put self-interest above His will. We avail ourselves of God's grace because we want to escape sin's domination over us. We are saved freely, without cost, by God's grace; but we turn to God's grace because we want Him to come into our lives and change us.

Grace is confused with sovereignty. Some say that because God alone is the author of salvation (and because He saves whom He will) we do not have to invite people to place their faith in Christ. Let it be stated emphatically that the sovereignty of God and salvation by grace fit together like a hand in a glove. It *is* God who saves. His Spirit enlightens our minds, convicts our hearts of sin, and draws us to Himself; but each person has the responsibility to believe. Faith is the human side of the coin. By faith, we respond to God's gracious offer.

We err by imagining that God's sovereign decrees negate the need for our decision making. Although God ultimately and mysteriously puts it on our hearts to respond to Him, we must be careful to warn others that God holds them responsible for choosing their destiny. God's ways are higher than ours. We will never be able to understand fully how God brings people to Himself until we get to heaven. In the meantime, we must confront people with the claims of Christ in such a straightforward way that they are acutely aware of the decision that is theirs to make. We cannot use salvation by God's grace as a cop-out to avoid our responsibility to tell others about Christ.

Our Gracious God

Earlier I said that God's grace is an otherworldly subject. People have a hard time understanding it, much less practicing it. Grace means that everything we need for life—fulfillment, union with God, and deliverance from sin—is offered to us freely and without cost to us through Jesus Christ. We experience God's grace by living in all the sufficiency of Christ. His death was sufficient to save us from the penalty of sin. His life within us is sufficient to deliver us from sin's power every day.

But why would God want to save us? Some say it is because He is kind. People can be kind to those they like, but our salvation is rooted in a quality found in God that people do not naturally possess. God is gracious. Grace is a favor lavished upon the totally undeserving and the utterly bankrupt.

Dr. Robert Ketchum used to tell the story of a wealthy man who was looking out of his living room window one day. He was happily enjoying the sight of his daughter swinging in the garden. She was surrounded by lovely flowers that almost defied description. The sight was totally pleasant to the father's eyes. Suddenly, a dirty, unkempt vagabond approaches the garden from off the street. He begins ripping out the flowers, destroying the lawn furniture, and polluting the garden pool. Then he sees the beautiful little girl. His eyes take on a special fury. He runs to her, seizes her, lifts her over his head, then dashes her to the pavement, killing her instantly. But he is not satisfied; he picks her up and throws her down over and over again until her little body is mutilated beyond recognition. Then, after his fury is spent, he sees the father looking in stunned disbelief out of the window. Slowly, he approaches the house carrying the battered girl in his arms. Horror seizes him as he realizes what he has done and what rightfully awaits him when the father opens the door. Smelly, sweaty, and bloody, he stands before the father and says, "Sir, I'm sorry."

If you were that father, what would you do? Scream for justice? Run for a gun? Kill him with your bare hands? Any of these responses might seem reasonable to us. But imagine that the father said, "I forgive you. Come into my house and live in my daughter's room. Let me bathe your wounds and give you some new clothes. Let me love you as I loved her. You are now my own!" That is grace to the undeserving.

Though all illustrations fall short of the true picture, I hope this story will help you appreciate the fact that we do not deserve God's favor; yet, through Christ, He has made it available to us. God is gracious. We are saved by grace. That God is free to be gracious is the triumph of the cross.

Thinking It Over

- Why is it important to bring people into an awareness of their guilt?
- How is pop psychology contributing to the problem of glossing over our guilt?
- What do we mean when we say that we are saved by grace?
- What is the chemistry of guilt and grace? How do these two concepts complement each other?
- In what way are guilt and grace triggers of the heart?

CHAPTER 4
When Evangelism Is a Way of Life

So they went on their way from the presence of the Council, rejoicing that they had been considered worthy to suffer shame for His name. And every day, in the temple and from house to house, they kept right on teaching and preaching Jesus as the Christ. (Acts 5:41-42)

Luke's account of the first evangelism explosion in the Book of Acts is certainly motivating! Who is not moved by this record of ordinary people who sincerely rejoiced that "they had been considered worthy to suffer shame for His name"? (Acts 5:41)

These early believers were gripped by a sense of destiny. They believed that they would live to see the day when the Good News penetrated every society. But do not be fooled; Acts is a book about realists. The people we read about were not ignorant of their weaknesses. Finding their strength in a message and convinced the Gospel could not fail, they suffered from no priority confusion. Nothing else they had or did really mattered! Add to this their willingness to suffer for their faith. Imagine the power that comes from a cause that is bigger than life itself. We read that their cause got its second wind after the first persecution. How do you stop people who are willing to die for what they believe?

These witnesses were not sidetracked by the prospect of political solutions to the problems of mankind. Although praying sincerely that service to the Lord could be rendered in an atmosphere of peace, they saw their ultimate task as saving people out of this world system. Study the Book of Acts and you will find not crusaders against slavery or political abuse, but rather a company who truly understood the distinction between heaven and earth. Instead of merely trying to reform a godless society, they fought to reconcile sinners to God. As converts multiplied, they committed themselves to each other in such a profound way that their very assemblies reflected a cultural alternative.

Much more could be said about the early saints who lived in such places as Rome, Antioch, Philippi, and Ephesus. The quality I admire most about them is their persistence. "Every day, in the temple and from house to house, *they kept right on* teaching and preaching Jesus as the Christ" (Acts 5:42, italics mine).

We should be cautious about building our doctrinal systems around narrative portions of Scripture (such as Acts) that portray events in history. Nevertheless, we can look for principles that are frequently repeated in these narratives. Here are some insights about evangelism drawn from recurring themes in the Book of Acts.

Evangelism: Sharing a Life-Changing Message with Others

The word *evangelism* comes from the Greek word for Gospel. Its core meaning is "good news from God." The Gospel is the good news of how God has provided a way of deliverance for people trapped in sin. The crux of the Christian Gospel is that Jesus Christ died for our sins (1 Cor. 15:3). This saving message doesn't end with the cross, though, for on the third day He rose from the grave.

The Gospel is a message to be believed. The angel said to Peter, "Go your way, stand and speak to the people in the temple the whole message of this Life" (Acts 5:20). The Gospel is a message to be believed about who Christ is and what He accomplished for us on the cross. We cannot believe in it without believing on Him! The evangelists in the Book of Acts would have been appalled by anyone who responded to their preaching by saying, "I believe Christ died for my sins and I want to go to heaven, but I don't want Him to interfere with the way I'm living my life."

Because the Gospel is a message to be believed, we understand faith as a positive response to what God has said and done through Christ. God acts or speaks and then asks, "What will you do with the message I have revealed to you?" By faith, we choose to depend personally on what God says. God initiates the process; we respond by believing.

Peter was warned by the Jewish authorities not to mention the name of Jesus. His response demonstrates his faith: "We must obey God rather than men. The God of our fathers raised up Jesus, whom you had put to death by hanging Him on a cross. He is the one whom God exalted to His right hand as a Prince and a Saviour, to grant repentance to Israel, and forgiveness of sins" (Acts 5:29-31). Peter heard the message, came to terms with Jesus Christ by faith alone, and staked his life on it. Christ was indeed Peter's Saviour and Lord.

Because the Gospel is a message to be believed, we are delivered from pursuing fleeting emotional experiences. The hope of this great Gospel message is as sure and as lasting as the once-for-all sacrifice of Christ and the eternal promise of God. In our day, much confusion stems from the misguided notion that we are saved by having some kind of religious experience. Rather than simply believing the message of the Gospel, frustrated seekers are trying to put faith in faith, or faith in repentance, or faith in their new attitudes. None of these will satisfy the heart. Our message must have Christ as its object rather than personal experiences.

Because the Gospel is a message to be believed, we understand evangelism as simply passing on this message to others. Luke says that after the first persecution in Jerusalem the saints were scattered and "those who had been scattered went about preaching the word" (Acts 8:4). These were not clergymen. These were butchers and bakers and businessmen. Although an "evangelist" is a person with a special gift and calling to preach the Gospel to the lost, the task of evangelism is shared by every member of the body of Christ. We can hardly improve on the definition of evangelism made popular by Campus Crusade for Christ: "Success in witnessing means taking the initiative to share Christ in the power of the Holy Spirit and leaving the results to God."

Because the Gospel is a message to be believed, the church is commanded to give every individual an opportunity to believe it. Perhaps the most quoted verse in Acts is this: "You shall receive power when the Holy Spirit has come upon you; and you shall be My witnesses both in Jerusalem, and in all Judea and Samaria, and even to the remotest part of the earth" (Acts 1:8). The early church realized they had been given a mandate to take the Gospel everywhere. And they did! This immense undertaking was bathed in prayer. After being warned to keep silent about the name of Jesus, the saints came together and prayed, "Lord, take note of their threats, and grant that Thy bond-servants may speak Thy word with all confidence" (Acts 4:29). God continually answered their prayers and opened doors. Luke continues, "And when they had prayed, the place where they had gathered together was shaken, and they were all filled with the Holy Spirit, and began to speak the word of God with boldness" (Acts 4:31).

Evangelism Is a Science
Evangelism is a science in that a fixed body of data is always present in a clear Gospel presentation. Study carefully the record in Acts. Count the references to Christ's crucifixion and resurrection. Situations, locations, and emphases were always changing, but the message remained the same. Here are the timeless themes that will always have to be proclaimed—the glory, personality, and holiness of God; the uniqueness and sinfulness of mankind; the redemptive work of the cross and the nature of the One crucified; and the responsibility we all have to place our faith in Christ.

Some, unfortunately, teach that the Book of Acts is a record of doctrinal transition and that its message changes as the book progresses. However, examination reveals that the message of the Gospel remains fixed throughout. Paul's final messages have the same theme as Peter's first sermons: "But I do not consider my life of any account as dear to myself, in order that I may finish my course, and the ministry which I received from the Lord Jesus, to testify solemnly of the gospel of the grace of God" (Acts 20:24).

Nineteen hundred years later, we must still take the time to master this data. How? In the same way we learned our geometry or chemistry. We must be willing to study and memorize and think. Let every would-be evangelist be clear about this! Many Christians are poor witnesses simply because they have lazy minds. I hope that by reading this book you will be persuaded there is much to learn.

Evangelism Is an Art

Evangelism is an art in that our personalities are always intrinsically involved in the evangelistic process. Just look at the contrasting styles of Peter and Paul. Each was unique in his vocabulary, temperament, mannerisms and customs, approach to his audience, and type of ministry. There are some things about your evangelistic approach that will set you apart from me, since no two people witness in exactly the same way. Don't try to become an evangelistic "clone" of some master evangelist. One of the most important keys of successful personal evangelism is to be yourself!

Evangelism is both a human activity and a divine activity. God is always at work when people are sharing their faith. It may appear that these men and women are the primary actors, but actually the real work of evangelism is taking place behind the scenes. When fruitful evangelism takes place, the Spirit of God uses our personalities and words to bring about His saving work. Paul witnessed to Lydia in Philippi, but we also read that "the Lord opened her heart to respond" (Acts 16:14).

God is at work when you share your faith. Take comfort in this, but do not let it become an excuse for poor preparation. Peter urges us always to be "ready to make a defense to every one who asks you to give an account for the hope that is in you" (1 Peter 3:15). Whether you are impulsive like Peter or logical like Paul, you must still master a reservoir of facts about redemption. God will then lead you to stress certain things and emphasize those aspects of the Gospel that especially impress you. Be sensitive to God's Spirit as He places upon your heart what truths and illustrations to highlight. Let Him use you to prepare the "soil" (Luke 8:15).

Methods of Evangelism

Joe Aldrich, in his helpful book *Life-Style Evangelism* (Multnomah), suggests that people evangelize in one of three ways. Not everyone could or should adopt the same method. Which is yours?

Proclamational evangelism. We refer to one person addressing many others in a public forum as a proclamation. Acts is full of evangelistic proclamations. After one of Peter's sermons, three thousand people turned to Christ (Acts 2:41). Now that's effective proclamation! In our day we might think of the ministry of Billy Graham (or perhaps that of your pastor) as an example of proclamational evangelism. It could be that that someone you know literally carries a soapbox and addresses crowds in the marketplace as does Brother Jed, who speaks regularly on the mall of the University of Wisconsin campus.

Although millions have been won to Christ through the ministry of proclamation evangelists, there are very few who have the gifts and calling to succeed here. If proclamational evangelism were God's only means of calling sinners to repentance, most of us would remain on the sidelines of evangelism.

Confrontational-intrusional evangelism. You have undoubtedly heard stories of people who witness to strangers on airplanes or who circulate around the neighborhood ringing doorbells; both of these are examples of confrontational, or intrusional, evangelism. The most popular kind of confrontational evangelism takes place in many churches on a regular basis. A few people take the visitors' cards from the previous week, get into their cars, and visit these people in their homes. When someone comes to the front door, the confrontation begins. Here is how Joe Aldrich describes this:

> Generally the "target audience" is a stranger. The limited time factor makes confrontation an immediate concern, and because no prior relationship usually exists, intrusion is neces-

sary before confrontation takes place. (pp. 78–79)

Jesus Christ confronted a woman at a well and a man watching from a tree. The Apostle Paul confronted King Agrippa and almost had him persuaded! A case can be made that the early believers actually did door-to-door evangelism (Acts 20:20). Such evangelism works well when hearts are prepared.

One difficulty with this method, though, is that not many Christians feel comfortable doing it. Aldrich believes that only a few in each congregation have this gift of evangelism. I know a fine pastor who looks for people who enjoy confrontational evangelism, and when he finds one, he suggests that this special liberty he or she has may define the gift of evangelism that is mentioned in Ephesians 4:11.

Another difficulty is that confrontational methods don't always take into account the nature of evangelism as a process. In this post-Christian society of ours, it takes time to demonstrate that Christ offers hope to people who have grown cynical. Most of us do not know our neighbors well enough to know their point of felt need. We must win the right to be heard, and this takes time.

Relational evangelism. The beauty of relational evangelism is that it grows out of everyday relationships and situations. Awkward encounters are minimized, and time, rather than being our enemy, is on our side. The Book of Acts ends with Paul being taken to Rome for trial.

Tragic? Not really, for the Lord was arranging some very special opportunities for relational evangelism. Paul shared Christ with the soldiers who guarded him day after day. He wrote about this unanticipated ministry to his Philippian friends: "Now I want you to know, brethren, that my circumstances have turned out for the greater progress of the gospel, so that my imprisonment in the cause of Christ has become well-known throughout the whole praetorian guard and to everyone else" (Phil. 1:12-13).

Do you feel imprisoned by circumstances at work? in your home? in your neighborhood? Take heart with Paul. Although he no longer had access to a soapbox, he could still share Christ naturally—over a long period of time with individuals.

On the Way to Conversion

While coming to know Christ, a person passes through various stages of thought. Let's call these stages "processes" and study four processes of thought involved in finding Christ.

The attraction process. This process involves alerting people who have spiritual needs to the fact that someone else has found some solutions through a relevant and appropriate demonstration. We have taken three chapters to make the point that demonstration precedes explanation. Let me simply offer a few examples. Our Lord captured the attention of the woman at the well by offering her "living water" (John 4:10); Peter got the ears of a whole city by healing a cripple; Paul told complete strangers at Athens that he had come to reveal the true identity of "the unknown God" they worshiped (Acts 17:23).

Do you worry about not being able to attract attention because you cannot perform the extraordinary wonders as did the apostles? Do not fret. Your life is the arena of quiet miracles. The Lord Jesus Christ is manifesting the fruit of the Spirit through *you.* Perhaps you have a quick mind and can arouse interest by talking about intriguing subjects. Maybe it is your servant's heart that will arrest attention. Sometimes it will be a very simple question, such as, "What comes into your mind when you ask yourself whether life has any ultimate meaning?"

The conviction process. This process involves helping people understand the seriousness of their sin predicament and their complete inability to solve the problem by themselves. I think some of the sterility of contemporary Christianity is grounded in a faulty understanding of salvation. It seems as though some think of salvation as something akin to having a date with Jesus, the superstar! From this perspective, knowing Jesus becomes nothing more than the frosting on the cake of an already satisfying life.

The reason people put their trust in Christ during the days of Peter and Paul was vastly different. Knowing they were in a desperate predicament and persuaded there was no other means of deliverance, they reached out to Christ in the same way a drowning child reaches out to his mother. Christianity offered hope only to the sick, the desperate, and the sinner.

If you understand that, you will understand the sermons in Acts. In almost every case, these sermons challenged listeners to face their guilt without rationalization or equivocation. When I read these great evangelistic messages, I learn about courageous people who were a far cry from entertainers who deliver syrupy messages to tickle their hearers' ears.

These early communicators probably spoke with tears in their eyes. They were straightforward but compassionate in declaring how serious the sin predicament really is. When the message is so candid, the response can be volatile. Some were moved by the Holy Spirit and joyously bowed the knee to Christ. But others scoffed, and still others became viciously hostile. As incredible as it seems, some people were so angered by this message that they left their jobs and followed the Apostle Paul from city to city trying to incite hatred toward him.

Only as we realize that salvation means deliverance will we become convinced of the necessity of communicating an accurate description of sin and its consequences. We must never lose sight of the truth that God's grace is available only to the guilty. Don't be surprised if it takes time for people to own up to their spiritual needs. The convicting work of the Holy Spirit is a subtle process.

The information process. Those who confess a spiritual problem are ready to come to terms with who Christ is and what He accomplished on the cross. In Acts 1:8 Jesus declares that He is at the center of the New Testament message. The Pentecost miracle is a testimony of Christ's triumphant exaltation. We find life through no other name (Acts 4:12); He is the Saviour of Israel, the Forgiver of her sins (Acts 5:31). Philip, the evangelist, preached Christ (Acts 8:5). Paul, in the euphoria of his recent conversion, said, "He is the Son of God. . . . Jesus is the Christ" (Acts 9:20, 22). Peter preached "peace through Jesus Christ (He is Lord of all)" (Acts 10:36). Paul told the Philippian jailer, "Believe in the Lord Jesus, and you shall be saved" (Acts 16:31).

These words caused considerable controversy in the first century, and Christianity continues to provoke intense opposition. Why? There are two principal reasons. Christians insist that Jesus Christ is *the only way* of salvation. Our message is shockingly exclusive. Second, Christians insist that (unlike all other religions) people must come to Christ in their *weakness*, not in their strength. Our message is a message of grace. We can come to God as we are only because Christ has done it all.

Jesus alone is the door. He is God's solution. He is the only hope of the world. He is the incomparable Christ. Is He the theme of your sharing? All of the real "fundamentals" of the faith concern Him: He was virgin born; He lived a sinless life; He died an atoning death; He rose bodily from the grave; He will come again as King of kings!

When Carol and I visited India, we were surprised to see pictures of Christ in every Hindu religious shop. We were told that Hindus have no problem accepting Christ as one of an endless number of gods. The group The Way sees Christ as a son of God just as we can be sons of God. Be careful about terminology. Preach the exclusive, all-sufficient, incomparable Christ in such a way that others can find genuine hope in His saving life.

The decision process. Ultimately we must help people realize that they need to make a decision. To become a Christian requires a definite act of the will. We have suddenly come to that part of evangelism that terrifies us! Many of us have no trouble talking about how Christ bridged the gap between sinful man and holy God, but our temperatures rise when we sense it is time to shift gears and ask, "What about you?"

In the evangelical church, we have seen the decision process take on circus characteristics. Lights are low and music is melodramatic. "Raise your hand—come kneel at the altar—now pray this prayer!" I often wonder if the packaging of the decision hasn't become more important than presenting a clear Gospel. Such packaging seems to deny that we truly believe salvation is of the Lord.

It was not so in the early church. We read of few altar calls and few prayers of decision in the Book of Acts. What we do find is people hearing a message, thinking it through, and then resting on it. This is what a decision for Christ is really all about. After Paul preached to the Athenians, people started making choices. "Now when they heard of the resurrection of the dead, some began to sneer, but others said, 'We shall hear you again concerning this.'...But some men joined him and believed" (Acts 17:32, 34).

Cornelius made a decision, but it was not an outward one. Peter was at the climax of his message (he hadn't even gotten to the altar call yet!) and was summarizing his convictions about Jesus Christ. In fact, Peter never finished that message! Cornelius and his friends believed Peter's words and slipped into the kingdom. Luke tells us, "While Peter was still speaking these words, the Holy Spirit fell upon all those who were listening to the message" (Acts 10:44).

I am not an expert on the decision process, but I am convinced that faith is a human response to divine truth revealed. Every time we hear the Word preached, we must respond. Sometimes we respond with a no and sometimes with a yes. Sometimes we say, "This is important. Please give me time to think it through."

Conversion usually involves the interplay of three personalities. First, there is the mysterious working of our sovereign God who opens the heart to respond (Acts 16:14). Next, there is God's messenger who brings truth to those in darkness (Acts 16:18). Finally, there is the decision of the hurting sinner who realizes that only Christ can meet his need (Acts 16:30).

Living in the Excitement of the Resurrection

For many years, I thought the Gospel could be summarized in these five words: "Christ died for our sins" (1 Cor. 15:3). But Paul does not end his sentence there. He goes on to say, "He was buried, and...He was raised on the third day" (v. 4).

Examine the Book of Acts carefully. You will be awestruck by the number of references to the resurrection of Christ. You may be tempted to dismiss these references as having little or no significance for the evangelistic enterprise. I confess to thinking such thoughts for many years, but now I am persuaded that a daily preoccupation with the resurrection is an indispensable ingredient in developing an evangelistic lifestyle.

Do you remember when the "God is dead" movement swept across America? Someone smartly and correctly observed that if God is dead, then death is God! Paul told the Corinthians, "If from human motives I fought with wild beasts at Ephesus, what does it profit me? If the dead are not raised, let us eat and drink for tomorrow we die" (1 Cor. 15:32).

Zeal for sharing Christ, especially in a hostile climate, grows out of one's ultimate view of this world. The resurrection changes everything here. If this life is all there is, then we might as well live these fleeting moments in a drunken stupor. But if Christ is alive—if Christ is *really* alive—there is a new world coming! Why aren't Christians today excited about evangelism? They are earthbound! This world and its many attractions are all we see. Because this is true, I sometimes wonder if there will ever again be an evangelism explosion of any magnitude in the Western world.

On the Day of Pentecost, Peter found all the power for living he would ever need in contemplating the meaning of Christ's resurrection. By it Christ was declared to be God, the grave was rendered powerless, and sin lost its grip on those who entered into Christ's resurrection life. When Peter believed the Gospel and received Christ into his life, even his fear of persecution and death was broken. He realized he was now a stranger on earth living in the last days of a doomed planet.

What does the reality of resurrection mean to me? The task of the church is not to try to impose heaven's ways on a bankrupt planet. Our mandate is to bring to all people a message about heaven. We are called out of the world system. Certainly we are to show kindness to needy people and to do what we can to help the poor and the needy; but if we really understand the prophetic Scriptures about the ominous future of our fallen planet, we will want to do more than meet physical needs. We will want to see sinners prepared for heaven. There can be no greater humanitarian impulse than to help others know God and join His forever family.

Dr. Dave Breese of Christian Destiny once spoke words to this effect: "Would you help me recapture the glow of a life consumed by Christ? Would you help me burn brightly with the flame of truth? Would you help me suffer willingly and courageously for Christ in a world of wicked men? Then sing me a song about heaven!"

In spite of untold obstacles, Paul never lost sight of resurrection reality. He explained what drove him to serve Christ to the Roman official Felix: "I do serve the God of our fathers . . . having a hope in God, which these men cherish themselves, that there shall certainly be a resurrection of both the righteous and the wicked. In view of this, I also do my best to maintain always a blameless conscience both before God and before men" (Acts 24:14-16).

Isn't it time for you to sing a song about heaven?

A Formula for Overcoming Our Fears

The contemporary evangelical church is almost paralyzed with fear. We fear ridicule: no one likes to be called a "religious nut"! This is my fear when I do open-air preaching on the university campus.

Another common fear has to do with questions people ask. We are just sure that people will ask us questions like, "Aren't good Hindus going to heaven? How come Christ didn't know the hour of His return? Does the Bible really teach that women are nothing but property? Why is it every Christian I know seems to be slightly neurotic?" (Remember, it is always easier to ask a religious question than it is to answer one. Learn how to answer such questions by asking another question.)

The list of fears is endless. Some people don't know how to begin a spiritual conversation. Others are afraid of talking to strangers. Some are afraid they are imposing their views on others. Still others do not want to turn people off to the Gospel by sharing poorly. What do you fear?

The Acts record gives us some timeless hints for overcoming our fears:

The early believers lived with a shared sense of awe. "They were continually devoting themselves to the apostles' teaching and to fellowship, to the breaking of bread and to prayer. And everyone kept feeling a sense of awe" (Acts 2:42-43). Every week (almost every day) they talked about what God was doing in and through them. There was no trace of defeatism in this spiritually supercharged atmosphere. Evangelism is a result of an entire fellowship encouraging each other—through worship, prayer, and teaching—to live for the Lord. Things are happening in churches that share a vision for God's ultimate priorities.

The early believers bore personal testimony to what Jesus Christ could do. "We cannot stop speaking what we have seen and heard" (Acts 4:20). The first-century world was not conquered by theologians and clergymen. It was penetrated by "uneducated and untrained men" (Acts 4:13). What set these people apart is that they were personally involved in what God was doing. We all know the danger of putting personal experience ahead of recorded truth, but it is equally dangerous to talk about religious abstractions that have never touched our lives. These early saints affirmed that Christ now lived within and was changing their attitudes and priorities. We are never afraid to talk about what we know firsthand!

The early believers conquered their fears only by facing real-life hostility. "They went on their way from the presence of the Council, rejoicing that they had been considered worthy to suffer shame for His name. And every day, in the temple and from house to house, they kept right on teaching and preaching Jesus as the Christ" (Acts 5:41-42). These verses stand out all the more when you read that before this they had been flogged and threatened. This incident was very important, for these Jerusalem saints now knew that they were willing to make any sacrifice for Christ. I think it is probably accurate to say that no one will overcome fear before facing a spiritual enemy and fighting a real battle. Not many of us today are willing to take advantage of opportunities to prove this to ourselves. These witnesses had tasted persecution and concluded that the Spirit living within would help them overcome any hardship. The victims emerged as the victors.

Leaders did not wait for long to involve new believers in evangelism. "And immediately he [Paul] began to proclaim Jesus in the synagogues" (Acts 9:20). The Christianity of the first century was a public movement. At first the Jerusalem believers continued to meet in the temple and never stopped talking about Jesus to the Jews there. The same thing happened in the synagogues of the principal cities of the area. Naturally, this public movement forced everyone to face their fears:

And at the hands of the apostles many signs and wonders were taking place among the people; and they were all with one accord in Solomon's portico. But none of the rest dared to associate with them; however, the people held them in high esteem. And all the more believers in the Lord, multitudes of men and women, were constantly added to their number. (Acts 5:12-14)

Luke records that people held the early saints in high regard, despite the fact that the Jewish authorities forbade them to associate with these zealous believers. Gradually individuals were so convinced of the truth of Christianity that they crossed the line and identified with this new movement in spite of the danger involved. There was no deadwood in the church. All had counted the cost and they shared their faith and encouraged each other continuously. As you read the Book of Acts, you will be amazed at how completely the fear of witnessing was overcome.

We must not underestimate how fearful people today are about sharing their faith. Because of these anxieties, people will not witness unless they are helped and encouraged by local groups of believers. Church evangelism programs ought to include training; friendship visitation; and a long-term, systematic involvement in community outreach. Only as churches build these components into their total programs will people be willing to face and overcome their fears of evangelism.

Involving new believers in evangelism will be relatively simple, but the greatest riddle in the church today is how to involve the established saints in outreach. God bless the church leadership team that is working creatively toward this end.

Thinking It Over
- In what way is evangelism both an art and a science?
- What are the three approaches to evangelism? With which one (if any) do you feel most comfortable?
- Why is the attraction process so important?
- Why is the resurrection an essential part of the Gospel?
- How did the first-century Christians deal with their fears about evangelism?

PART TWO

What Will It Take?

A
Message!

PROLOGUE TO PART TWO
A SYSTEMATIC STUDY OF THE GOSPEL OF CHRIST

Two verses in Paul's letter to the Galatians amaze me. Paul says, "Grace to you and peace from God our Father, and the Lord Jesus Christ, who gave Himself for our sins, that He might deliver us out of this present evil age, according to the will of our God and Father" (1:3-4). In a few short words, Paul summarizes the whole Gospel message. Christ died on the cross to save us from our sins and to set us apart from a corrupt world system that is in rebellion against God. What could be clearer?

Yet in the same passage Paul writes, "I am amazed that you are so quickly deserting Him who called you by the grace of Christ, for a different gospel" (1:6). He is aware that these Galatians are being seduced by false teachers, and he soberly announces a curse on anyone who subverts the Gospel (1:8). He shared a similar fear about subversion with the Corinthians: "I am afraid, lest as the serpent deceived Eve by his craftiness, your minds should be led astray from the simplicity and purity of devotion to Christ" (2 Cor. 11:3).

It appears that the Gospel is both simple and subvertible! We subvert it by adding our work to what God has already accomplished perfectly on the cross. From the earliest period of the church, some have attempted to make salvation a human work. In Acts 15:1 we read about those who said, "You can't be saved if you're not circumcised!" Today some are saying, "You can't be saved if you're not baptized!"

We will do well to study the New Testament Gospel of grace with diligence. What was it about this great message that set men free? How did it transform lives? How can we avoid the subtle danger of attaching strings and conditions to this unconditional invitation to know God? How can we guard against an "easy believism" that sees Christianity merely as a creed to affirm?

Chapter 5 will provide biblical undergirding for the Gospel message we share. Nothing in this book is more important than this. There is power and authority in the Word of God. May God challenge you to develop your entire Gospel presentation from the Scriptures, for the Holy Spirit uses the Word to bring conviction.

Chapter 6 speaks to the question, "Are there two Gospels?" Is the Gospel in the Old Testament different from the Gospel of grace that dominates the New Testament? If you're frustrated, wondering if God changed His plans halfway through history, this important chapter is for you.

This unit concludes with an explanation of what it means to be justified by faith. The Gospel is the story of what God, in Christ, has done to provide redemption for fallen man. How do we respond to this revelation? What does it mean to place our faith in Christ? What do we mean when we say that we are justified by faith? Answers to these questions will help you share your faith more effectively.

CHAPTER 5
The Four Crucial Issues

"This is eternal life, that they may know Thee, the only true God." (John 17:3)

Evangelical Christianity holds as its major premise that God has broken through to us, revealing everything we must know to live abundantly and eternally. The real wonder of this revelatory miracle is that we finite people can make sense of it! Because of the Bible, people can come to terms with eternal truth. What God has revealed about the pathway of life eternal transcends every cultural barrier.

Because God has revealed Himself through the Bible and because He has definitely stated on what terms He can be known, the Gospel is an objective message. It has as its theme *knowing God.* Jesus Himself said, "This is eternal life, that they may know Thee, the only true God, and Jesus Christ whom Thou hast sent" (John 17:3). Because sin keeps us from knowing God, the sin problem first has to be resolved. Christ came into the world to break through the sin barrier so we might know God.

Our Gospel is valid only if it is the message of the Scriptures. The purpose of this chapter is to present a biblical basis for every thought we seek to share through the *Evangelism Encounter* methodology. What follows is an attempt to substantiate the four principle components of the Gospel from the Bible. I call these components the four crucial issues because they are the irreducible core of the Gospel.

Life's Secret: Each of Us Was Born with a Need to Know God

The Book of Romans has always held a special place in Christian theology. It was given first place among the epistles by the early church fathers, and with good reason. It is Paul's great theological treatise on the way of salvation. Romans is a book that cannot be ignored by Christ's witnesses. It presents us with vital information that can help us share Christ's Good News.

What is the flow of Paul's thought? He begins with man's need to know God. Paul's insight into the human predicament begins with his declaration that human beings have an intrinsic awareness that God exists (1:19). Incredibly, they choose to suppress this knowledge (1:18), attaching higher value to autonomy than to living purposefully under divine rule.

Do not miss the point. The epistle begins with our need to know God. So many of our Gospel presentations begin with the declaration that God loves us, but until we fully understand what we are like apart from God, we will not be moved by God's love for us. Paul does not even introduce the theme of God's love until the fifth chapter of Romans.

Why do people deny their need for God? "They did not honor Him as God" (1:21). In other words, they chafed at the thought of their divine accountability. They also refused to "give thanks" to God. That is, they refused to acknowledge that their minds and bodies, personalities and skills were really gifts from God. They not only repudiated divine ownership; they rejected the thought of being debtors to the Almighty.

What happens when people deny their need to know God? On a purely psychological level human life loses its significance. When man puts himself in the center of the universe—when man becomes the measure of all things—truth becomes the measure of all things. Truth becomes relative, and might makes right. To quote Paul again: "They became futile in their speculations" (1:21). All human laws and values became arbitrary because there was no absolute standard to which one could appeal.

Moreover, "their foolish heart was darkened." It was not just our reasoning processes that were affected by the decision to suppress all truth of God. Our moral sensitivities were likewise affected. People began to crave the very things that should have repulsed them. Newly autonomous, man declared himself "liberated" and "enlightened" and so betrayed his own foolishness (1:22). By exchanging the glory of God for an image in the form of corruptible man, these pitiable fools became like their new gods. They became brute beasts (1:24-32).

The same apostle gave an enlightening sermon to the Athenians. This message, recorded in Acts 17, is noteworthy because it helps us to see how Paul began a Gospel presentation to those who had no Judeo-Christian heritage. He begins by declaring that our need for God is undeniable.

> The God who made the world and all things in it, since He is Lord of heaven and earth, does not dwell in temples made with hands; neither is He served by human hands, as though He needed anything, since He Himself gives to all life and breath and all things; and He made from one, every nation of mankind to live on all the face of the earth, having determined their appointed times, and the boundaries of their habitation, that they should seek God, if perhaps they might grope for Him and find Him, though He is not far from each one of us; for in Him we live and move and exist, as even some of your own poets have said, "For we also are His offspring." (Acts 17:24-28)

Paul stresses that the Athenians (along with everyone else) were designed in such a way that they should seek God. You and I are just the same. God made us to need Him. Deny this need and life stops making sense. Deny this need and we become like brute beasts.

Evangelism begins by helping people recognize that they have this need. But what can we say to people who insist that it is difficult for them to believe in God? For sooner or later you will be asked, "But how can we be sure that God exists? After all, no one can see Him. What kind of evidence makes you so sure that

God is real?"

When confronted by such questions, we must honestly confess that we cannot prove that God exists. If we could prove God's existence scientifically, no faith on our part would be necessary, and God wants us to live by faith. To be sure, faith is not make-believe. Things are not true simply because we wish them to be true. By faith we grasp hold of invisible realities that leave "footprints" that we can observe through reason.

What are some of these "footprints"? Consider first our own *human nature*. The Bible declares that mankind is unique. We were created for a special purpose—to be expressions of God's personality, extensions of His presence, and exhibitions of His power (Gen. 1:27-28). As such, we have a *spiritual* nature. We are set apart from all other beings because we are made in God's image. King David realized this when he said, "I will give thanks to Thee, for I am fearfully and wonderfully made" (Ps. 139:14). In Psalm 8 David looks out over the entire expanse of the universe and marvels that God has a special interest in the creatures who inhabit one tiny planet: "What is man that Thou dost take thought of him?" (v. 4)

Each of us has a spiritual essence. This explains why we all share in the pursuit of love, purpose, and immortality. It explains why only human beings and not animals think about such sublime abstractions as justice, mercy, beauty, joy, and peace. And by such reasoning we are forced to wonder, "Why have You made me thus?"

Our entire beings cry out in perfect awareness that we are more than just molecules in motion. We have a spiritual nature. This makes no sense at all apart from a spiritual Designer! We bear the unmistakable stamp of God's personality upon our lives.

Consider also the "footprint" of *human history*. When we open the books and read through the dusty pages of the past, we see the enigma of human history. From the beginning governments talk of peace but usually end up at war. Why? Because selfishness and peacefulness are mutually exclusive (James 4:1-2). God did not create us to be selfish, but He gave us the power of choice.

We learn from history that people continually use their power of choice selfishly and therefore live in perpetual conflict. War between peoples has its root in the war of the soul. How does this sad story of human history confirm the existence of a good and loving God? It explains why people long for happiness but end up in misery. God created us to know and love Him; He gave us the capacity to choose to live in fellowship with Him. Instead, we use our power of choice to further our own selfish ends. When we do this, everyone suffers. Ironic, isn't it, that even man's inhumanity to man only confirms that a loving God must exist.

Finally, consider the "footprint" of the *natural universe.* This world of wonder and order is an eloquent testimony to God's genius. "For since the creation of the world His invisible attributes, His eternal power and divine nature, have been clearly seen, being understood through what has been made, so that they are without excuse" (Rom. 1:20). Does God really exist? Take a careful look at the world around you. The psalmist says: "The heavens are telling of the glory of God; and their expanse is declaring the work of His hands" (Ps. 19:1).

If there is such overwhelming evidence for God, why are there so many skeptics and atheists in our world? Personally, I believe that atheism is learned behavior. Kids have a natural interest in God. It's intuitive. Then something happens. Circumstances appear to turn against us. Grief turns to bitterness, and bitterness turns to denial. Such denial is a foolish and immature response to human pain. No wonder it is only "the fool" who says, "There is no God" (Ps. 14:1). The Apostle Paul tells us that some deny God because their hearts are hard (Eph. 4:18). Hard hearts give way to willful ignorance. Such ignorance leads to intellectual futility. When people can no longer make sense out of life with their minds, they turn to their passions for satisfaction (Eph. 4:19). Paul's insightful description sounds much like the Western world at the end of the twentieth century.

Mankind's Problem: Our Sinfulness Keeps Us from Knowing God

The conviction that God must exist leads to a more pressing question. If God created us, why are we so unfulfilled? Spend three minutes in any great city of the world today and you will conclude that we have a problem.

We are no longer the way God created us. The race came into existence when God fashioned a beautiful man and woman who loved each other very much. They lived in innocence and contentment in an ideal environment, the place called Eden. Almost immediately this original pair came under the seductive influence of the prince of darkness. This serpent deceived Eve and encouraged Adam to sin. As a result, the human race fell into rebellion against God. Ever since, people have been running away from God. We subconsciously say to Him, "I want my own way; I can live my life without Your help. Don't interfere with my plans!"

We may not want to admit it, but humanity's essential problem is spiritual, not economic. People want to live autonomously. Most people don't think they are rebelling against God. They do not see themselves as slaves to their selfish desires. At one time, the Apostle Paul felt this way also. He thought of himself as a pretty good guy, doing "just fine" on his own, until he read what the Bible said about coveting (Rom. 7:7-9). For the first time, it dawned on him that all of his religion was just an expression of personal pride. We are like this as well. We think we can authenticate ourselves through personal accomplishment, which may almost convince us that we have no spiritual needs.

Popular views about sin. If we are going to be effective in sharing our faith, we must help people see through the deceptive smoke screen of their own accomplishments. We must lovingly communicate the true nature of our sin problem. Ask people on the street how they view human sin and they will almost invariably share two ideas with you. First, they will describe sin as an activity, such as stealing or being disrespectful to parents. The villagers called Zaccheus a "sinner" because he cheated the people into paying high taxes (Luke 19:7).

Because of this perception, most people believe they have the capacity to deal with their sin. "If ever I wanted to get serious about my sin, I could solve the problem!" How? The plan may include going back to church, reading a good self-actualization book, exercising moral resolve, or turning over a new leaf. In

Luke's Gospel, a young ruler thought that his conduct was good enough to earn him a place in heaven (18:21). He was not so bad; he could solve his own problems. Most of us tend to think the same way.

These notions are not biblical. In reality our actions are only the tip of the iceberg. The sin situation is far more complicated. We sin because we have a sinful nature (Jer. 17:9). Sin is a condition of the heart by which we demand our own way (Isa. 53:6). We live in a state of subtle rebellion against God's rightful rule over our lives.

Now comes the sobering part. The Bible assures us that humanly speaking, there is *absolutely no cure* for this attitude. Sin is pictured in the Bible as a wretched cancer that ultimately destroys us (Isa. 1:6). Isaiah declares that every attempt to cure the sin problem through our own devices only smudges up our sin stains and makes them worse (64:6).

Sin's serious consequences. Not only is the sin predicament incurable, but sin produces predictable and devastating consequences (Gal. 6:7-8). We live in a cause-and-effect universe. No one really gets away with sinful activity. Our sinfulness keeps us from knowing God. Sin cuts us off from God, others, and even from ourselves.

Never have people been more prosperous than they are in the Western world today. Incredibly, many are using this new wealth to destroy themselves. The widespread abuse of drugs, sex, and alcohol is ample proof that people are trying to escape the frustrations of their own inner lives. People are unwilling to deal with the root problem of sin. What are the consequences of sin? We can best identify them in three ways:

Sin cuts us off from ourselves. The *psychological* consequence of sin is realized through the boredom of an *empty* life (Ecc. 1:2). Go to a high school or university in America today and you will hear someone complaining to a roommate or counselor, "I wish I could get my act together." Psychologists often counsel patients who express their problem as a gut-level feeling of self-hatred. Hatred produces the impulse to destroy. So many young people are insecure and unsure of themselves. Realizing they are somehow incomplete, they confess to a void they can't fill.

Sin cuts us off from others. We must also face the *social* consequences of sin. Sinful people feel alone in a crowd, and lonely people are bitter people. As I write, fighting is going on for the supremacy of Beirut, Lebanon. On paper, the solution seems possible. Christians and Moslems ought to respect each other's rights. In this real world, however, it is not that easy. There is a little Beirut in every corner of the world. Human beings of different perspectives, race, or status feel alone and alienated from each other. When people feel unloved, they strike out at others through bitterness, hatred, and fear.

Sin cuts us off from God. Sinners must ultimately face the *spiritual* consequences of sin (Eph. 5:6). The wages of sin is *death,* and spiritual death means that we are cut off from God (Rom. 6:23). Our holy and just God cannot tolerate sin in His presence, but because He created us for fellowship, we have an inner need for reconciliation. The biblical description of what happens to those who die in their sin is not pretty (Luke 16:19-31). I think this is the principal reason many reject the Bible. Our minds do not want to conceive of the possibility of being cut off from God forever. However, the Bible assures us that hell is a real place. God created it for Satan and his demons (Matt. 25:41). He places obstacle after obstacle on the path that leads to destruction (Rom. 10:21), for He desires "all men to be saved and to come to the knowledge of the truth" (1 Tim. 2:4). Still, He gives us the right to refuse His love (Matt. 23:37). The Scriptures paint a fearful picture of the ultimate state of those who continue to rebel against God:

> The Lord Jesus shall be revealed from heaven with His mighty angels in flaming fire, dealing out retribution to those who do not know God and to those who do not obey the gospel of our Lord Jesus. And these will pay the penalty of eternal destruction, away from the presence of the Lord and from the glory of His power. (2 Thes. 1:7-9)

God's Solution: God Loved Us Enough to Send His Son, Jesus Christ, to Die on the Cross to Pay for Our Sins

"I am sorry, but there is no cure." Words cannot express the chilling effect this statement has had upon countless families. Dedicated surgeons are always looking for an acceptable way to inform loved ones that the patient has an inoperable malignancy.

"No cure": we find it difficult even to frame the words. But until we can accept this truth about our human predicament, we will not waste our time looking for God's solution.

When we share Christ, we must first state clearly that humanly speaking, there is no cure for our sin predicament. We have then set the stage for a wonderful announcement—*God has a solution!* He alone is the source of our salvation. He has found a way that we can know deliverance from sin and its consequences.

To be able to appreciate the splendor of God's solution, we must imagine a divine dilemma. No one can pay for the consequences of his own sin and live, for the Bible teaches that the penalty for our sin is death (Rom. 6:23). How, then, can sinners pay for their sins and remain alive? The solution is found in Jesus Christ. Listen to the Scriptures: "Since the children [humankind] have flesh and blood, He [Christ] too shared in their humanity so that *by His death* He might destroy him who holds the power of death—that is, the devil—and free those who all their lives were held in slavery by their fear of death" (Heb. 2:14-15, NIV, italics mine). The penalty and consequences of sin are so deeply embedded in every human heart that they cannot be removed by religious rites, moral reformations, or superficial attempts at a new life. Jesus is the answer. There is no other.

The deity of Christ. Who is Jesus Christ? Undoubtedly this is the watershed issue of Christianity. Not surprisingly, Christ's deity has been fiercely debated through the centuries. Think for a moment how the cultists cringe at the announcement that Jesus Christ is "very God of very God." No doctrine of Christianity is more important; no declaration draws such heavy fire from unbelievers.

Why are we convinced that Christ was truly God? Isaiah said that the coming Messiah would be the "Mighty God" (9:6). John 1:1 says that Christ (the Word) was God. This "Word" became flesh! All that God is became localized in a body. In Matthew 22:41-46, Christ Himself defended His divinity by quoting a prophetic psalm in which King David spoke of the Messiah as his

Lord (Ps. 110:1). Christ forces detractors to come to terms with His unique identity. Christ told the woman at the well that He was the Messiah (John 4:26). He boldly announced that He would give eternal life to His followers (John 10:28). He startled His listeners when He said, "Before Abraham was born, I AM" (John 8:58). Just as shocking were His words in John 8:24, "Unless you believe that I am He, you shall die in your sins." And in John 10:30, Jesus said, "I and the Father are one."

Christ has the prerogatives of deity. In John 5, Christ declares His deity by claiming two prerogatives of deity. First, He has the divine *authority to give life* to whomever He wills (v. 21). He declares that He can raise people from the dead. Second, He informs His listeners that He alone has the *authority to judge men and forgive sins* (v. 27). Certainly, Christ was not confused about His identity! Either He was deceived (a lunatic), or deceitful (a liar), or deity (the Lord).

Christ is the biblical object of worship. The Father in heaven suffers no confusion about Christ's identity. If you study Hebrews 1, you will be struck by the clarity of the Heavenly Father's view of Christ. The chapter comes to a climax in verse 6 where God commands the angels of heaven to fall down before the Son of God and worship Him. Such words are extraordinary when one remembers God's hatred of idolatry and His zeal to be worshiped exclusively.

Jesus Christ was God. He did not become God; He always was God. He existed as God from eternity past; yet, at a precise moment in time and space, He became a man. Why?

The death of Christ. The Old Testament set the stage for the coming and dying of Jesus Christ. Consider four ways it pointed to Calvary. The first promise of Genesis is that Eve's seed (Christ) would ultimately triumph over Satan and sin, but it would be a painful victory. The Lord said to the serpent, "He shall bruise you on the head and you shall bruise him on the heel" (3:15). At Calvary, Christ administered to Satan a mortal wound and triumphed over him despite the pain of the cross.

The Old Testament also set the stage for our understanding of salvation as deliverance through shed blood. God engineered the release of the nation of Israel from Egyptian bondage through ten devastating plagues. The last plague was the death of all the firstborn in the land. The people were given only one hope—to sprinkle lamb's blood and "I will pass over you" (Ex. 12:13). This national deliverance through blood was a picture of how God delivers us from death through the sacrifice of Jesus Christ. Paul told the Corinthians that Christ was our "Passover" (1 Cor. 5:7).

Calvary is also seen in the provision of blood sacrifices. The Book of Leviticus was written to help God's people understand that their sins made it impossible for a Holy God to fellowship with them as they were. To correct this problem, priestly sacrifices were instituted. These animal sacrifices were a temporary covering (atonement) for the sins of the people. God accepted them because He knew that Christ would ultimately die for the sins of the whole world (Rom. 3:25). These animal sacrifices were vivid illustrations of the principle of *substitution.* "He shall lay his hand on the head of the burnt offering, that it may be *accepted for him* to make atonement on his behalf" (Lev. 1:4, italics mine). In the same way, Jesus Christ died as our substitute, "the just for the unjust" (1 Peter 3:18).

Another annual event described in the Book of Leviticus helps us to understand the cost of our redemption. Consider the story of the scapegoat:

> Then Aaron shall lay both of his hands on the head of the live goat, and confess over it all the iniquities of the sons of Israel, and all their transgressions in regard to all their sins; and he shall lay them on the head of the goat and send it away into the wilderness by the hand of a man who stands in readiness. And the goat shall bear on itself all their iniquities to a solitary land; and he shall release the goat in the wilderness. (Lev. 16:21-22)

In these verses, we read about one sin-bearing animal cut off from the nation. The priest put his hands on the goat, symbolically transferring the sins of the people to the animal. This creature was then driven deep into the wilderness. The scapegoat illustrates how Jesus Christ bore in His own body the ultimate consequence for our sin. At Calvary, He was cut off *physically,* for He died a real death. Because all who watched His shame mocked His helplessness, he was cut off *socially*. But the Saviour's greatest agony was that He was cut off *spiritually;* for when He died for our sins, God Almighty turned His back on Him.

Now let's examine the New Testament record. Consider the day that Christ died. He hung on the cross for six hours. The first three hours He endured the wrath of man. The last three hours He endured the wrath of God. This final period began at noon when the sky turned black as coal (Matt. 27:45). Everyone was terrified. Christ alone understood what was happening.

The blackness of the sky signaled the abandonment of Christ by the Father. We must try to understand the emotional trauma that Jesus experienced just then. From eternity past, Jesus Christ lived in unbroken unity and equality with His Father. Now, He was cut off. No wonder He cried out, "My God, My God, why hast Thou forsaken Me?" (Matt. 27:46) This was Christ's death scream. He was tasting death for each of us (Heb. 2:9).

The central fact of our faith is that Jesus Christ died for us. He became a man so that He could die a substitutionary death for mankind. Consider how many verses in the Bible speak of Christ's substitutionary work:

Matthew 26:28: "This is My blood of the covenant, which is to be shed on behalf of many for forgiveness of sins."
Mark 10:45: "[Christ came] to serve, and to give His life a ransom for many."
Luke 24:26: "Was it not necessary for the Christ to suffer these things?"
John 3:14: "As Moses lifted up the serpent in the wilderness, even so must the Son of Man be lifted up [crucified]."
John 10:11: "The good shepherd lays down His life for the sheep."
Romans 4:25: "[Christ] was delivered up [to the cross] because of our transgressions."
Romans 5:8: "While we were yet sinners, Christ died for us."
1 Corinthians 15:3: "Christ died for our sins according to the Scriptures."

2 Corinthians 5:21: "He made Him who knew no sin to be sin on our behalf."

Colossians 1:20: "Through Him to reconcile all things to Himself, having made peace through the blood of His cross."

1 Timothy 2:6: "[Jesus Christ] gave Himself as a ransom for all."

Hebrews 2:9: "He might taste death for everyone."

Hebrews 9:26: "He has been manifested to put away sin by the sacrifice of Himself."

Hebrews 9:28: Christ was "offered once to bear the sins of many."

Hebrews 10:12: "But He, having offered one sacrifice for sins for all time, sat down at the right hand of God."

1 Peter 1:19: You were redeemed "with precious blood, as of a lamb unblemished and spotless, the blood of Christ."

1 Peter 2:24: "He Himself bore our sins in His body on the cross."

1 Peter 3:18: "Christ . . . died for sins once for all, the just for the unjust."

1 John 1:7: "The blood of Jesus His Son cleanses us from all sin."

1 John 2:2: "He Himself is the propitiation [satisfaction] for our sins."

Revelation 1:5: "To Him who loves us, and released us from our sins by His blood."

The Scriptures also emphasize that the saving work of Jesus Christ has been completed. He perfectly accomplished His task. No wonder He shouted, "It is finished!" just before He bowed His head and yielded His spirit.

The resurrection of Christ. Although Christ's death is central to salvation, the Bible never leaves Christ nailed to the cross. We must consider three vital implications of Christ's resurrection.

The resurrection affirms deity. In the Scriptures, the doctrine of the bodily resurrection of Christ is usually (and properly) linked to the question, "Why do we believe that Christ is really God?"

Romans 1:4 tells us that Jesus Christ was declared to be the

Son of God in a powerful way by the resurrection from the dead. When the hostile leaders asked Christ for a supernatural sign of His authority (see Matthew 12:38-41), Christ responded by announcing that one sign would be given—His death, burial, and resurrection. We believe in the divinity of Christ because He alone conquered the grave and rose triumphant on the third day.

The resurrection confirms success. Christ's resurrection is also a confirmation of the success of His saving death on the cross. Romans 4:25 says that Christ "was raised because of [on account of] our justification." How could Christ's followers be sure that Christ's sacrificial death was a sufficient payment for the sins of all humanity? How is our confidence enhanced by our knowledge of Christ's resurrection?

Imagine how confused you would feel if Christ told you He was God and was going to die for your sins but that after His death, His body just rotted in a grave. You could never really be sure that your problem was solved.

God raised Jesus Christ from the dead to provide us with that assurance! Belief in Christ was not left to chance. The early apostles brought the message of the Gospel to all people everywhere because they had seen the risen Christ. They had no more questions. Not only were they satisfied, they lost all their fears. No longer afraid to die, they were now ready to live.

Your Responsibility: You Can Come to Know God Personally by Placing Your Trust in Jesus Christ as Your Saviour and Lord

I recently returned from a month of evangelistic ministry in Europe. As my wife, Carol, and I traveled through Belgium, we commented that it was probably impossible to stand on any square acre of that entire country and not view a church spire. In each church can be found graphic reminders of Christ's crucifixion. Crosses, statues, and paintings depict Christ's passion. The people who attend these churches must know all about the fact that Christ died for their sins. Yet there is a spiritual bondage throughout that continent that is troubling. How can we explain this irony?

We must ask the question, "Why do so many people who say

they believe in Jesus Christ feel so unsure about their relationship with God?" The answer to this question has to do with the way we define *faith.* Most people equate faith with knowledge. If you were to ask the people of Belgium whether they believe in Jesus Christ, most would certainly say, "Of course! When I was young, I went to church to get confirmed and studied the catechism and learned all about Him!" But saving faith is more than this. Consider three biblical propositions about faith.

Faith as personal choice. Part of what it means to be created in God's image is that we have the capacity to choose our destiny. Mysteriously, this human power of choice ultimately meshes with God's sovereign will. Paul told the Thessalonians, "God has chosen you from the beginning for salvation through sanctification by the Spirit and *faith in the truth*" (2 Thes. 2:13, italics mine). In the next verse, we read that God "called you through our gospel." Put these ideas together and you will be convinced that when we share Christ, we are informing our listeners that a choice must be made.

One of the most powerful pictures in the Old Testament is the contest between Elijah and 850 false prophets. Elijah demanded that two sacrifices be prepared, one to Baal and one to Jehovah. "The God who answers by fire" and consumes the sacrifice would be recognized as the only true God (1 Kings 18:24). Elijah comes to the crux of the challenge with these words: "How long will you hesitate between two opinions? If the Lord is God, follow Him; but if Baal, follow him" (18:21).

We are missing the mark if we share Christ without persuading our listener to make a decision. The New Testament preachers made this crystal clear. On the Day of Pentecost, Peter begged his listeners, "Be saved from this perverse generation!" (Acts 2:40) Through Paul the Athenians were convicted with this personal exhortation, "God is now declaring to men that all everywhere should repent" (Acts 17:30).

God will pardon all who come to Him through Jesus Christ. Paul teaches, "Whoever will call upon the name of the Lord will be saved" (Rom. 10:13). We are on target when we insist that saving faith always involves a person's will. The Bible speaks of believing from the "heart" (Rom. 10:10), but this always refers to the control center of a person rather than the seat of one's emotions.

Can this decision process be distilled into a single idea? I think so. Here is one way to present the decision:

> Recognizing that I have a sin problem that I cannot solve by myself and understanding that Jesus Christ died on the cross to pay for my sins, I now place my trust in Jesus Christ alone as my Saviour and Lord.

Faith as total dependence. Faith is a dependence on what God says that is so real that our outlook changes dramatically. Paul in Romans 4:21 defines faith as complete dependence upon what God has promised. If you want to get to the bottom line of Christianity, ask the questions, What am I really depending on to save me? In what is my hope? The writer of Hebrews tells us that the only satisfactory anchor for the soul is the truth God has revealed in His Word (6:18). Remember the little Gospel chorus? "Christ did it! God said it! I believe it! That settles it!"

When our Lord explained faith to His disciples, He invited a small child to sit on His lap. He then said, "Truly, I say to you, unless you are converted and become like children, you shall not enter the kingdom of heaven" (Matt. 18:3). Children have no difficulty at all depending on their parents for all their needs. Nor are they suspicious of what parents say. Children have a natural capacity to believe what their fathers tell them. Christian faith centers on our capacity to believe what God says to us about His Son, Jesus Christ. Will we choose to depend on Christ or on ourselves?

Faith as acceptance of Christ's lordship. Paul wrote, "No one can say 'Jesus is Lord,' except by the Holy Spirit" (1 Cor. 12:3). For Paul, the lordship of Christ was both the starting point and the goal of Christianity. As the starting point, one must recognize that Christ is his rightful Lord. Paul did this on the Damascus Road after he encountered the risen Christ unexpectedly. He said, "Lord, what do You want me to do?"

Do you see that recognizing Christ as Lord is an act of faith? This personal acknowledgment is simply coming to terms with who Christ really is. So many of us are afraid to talk about Christ's lordship when we witness. We think it sounds as if we are asking someone to clean up his life and therefore "work" for his salvation.

We are not converted by changing our lifestyle. But what is conversion? Once we were content to do everything our way. Living only for ourselves is the heart of our sin problem. In so living we gradually saw how trapped and unfulfilled we had become. Then, we heard the Good News. We were told about a way out. We could find deliverance from sin by trusting Christ. We acknowledged that we were dead without Him and that we could enter into life only by giving our lives to Him. Salvation is deliverance from the pathetic condition of living for self-interest.

But make no mistake—Paul did not have his act together when he trusted Christ. In fact, at the end of his life he still lamented his lack of perfection. If eternal life could be earned, Paul would be forever lost. But as one who understood the goodness and grace of Christ, it was his desire to practice a truer submission to the lordship of Christ with each passing day.

Before we invite our listeners to put their trust in Christ, it might be helpful to say:

We don't earn eternal life by changing our lifestyles, but somehow, after we give Christ the right to lead us, our lives do change. It's important that you realize that you are putting your trust in Jesus Christ as your Lord. I just want you to understand that Jesus Christ is not an absentee God. He wants to be in constant communion with you. He wants to guide you into an abundant life. The only way that any believer can be at peace and experience true, inner contentment is to obey Christ.

Christianity is so much more than just mumbling a creed or signing a doctrinal statement that never penetrates our hearts. We enter the kingdom when we affirm the words of the old hymn: "King of my life I crown Thee now!" This is why the world rejects Christ. You can understand why there are so few true believers, the pride in each of us stubbornly resists this transfer of authority. How we fight against giving Christ the right to take control! But this is completely consistent with what faith demands, for faith stands on what the Bible tells us concerning Christ. Who is He? He is both Saviour and Lord! At the moment of conversion we enter into a covenant agreement with Him. We give Him our permission to take over our lives.

Now, let me summarize saving faith by uniting these three propositions about faith into a single sentence: Saving faith is choosing to depend on Christ alone as Saviour (because He died for our sins on the cross) and choosing to relate to Him as Lord (because He rose from the dead and is now seated on God's throne).

Thinking It Over
- How would you defend the proposition that each of us was born with a need to know God?
- What are two common misconceptions about sin?
- Why is the cross so crucial to our presentation of the Gospel?
- What is the difference between the world's definition of faith and that of the Bible?

CHAPTER 6
One Saving Message throughout the Scriptures

But now apart from the Law the righteousness of God has been manifested, being witnessed by the Law and the Prophets. (Romans 3:21)

And if you belong to Christ, then you are Abraham's offspring, heirs according to promise. (Galatians 3:29)

You may have heard a Moslem say, "I believe that Jesus Christ was a great prophet, but Mohammed is God's final prophet." Adherents of the Baha'i faith go a step further by insisting that Bahaullah is God's ninth and ultimate messenger.

Such prophets have introduced false doctrines that contradict the great saving themes of the Bible, but they force us to consider a difficult question. Didn't Jesus Christ Himself bring a saving message that contradicted the Old Testament message of salvation? Is the saving message of the Old Testament different from the Good News taught by Paul? This is an important subject, and if we are going to master the doctrine of salvation, we must be willing to face it.

The Gospel of the Covenant in the Old Testament
The centrality of faith. Faith has always been central to God's saving plan. Abraham was the father of the nation of Israel. His personal experience of coming to terms with God would set a

precedent for all the Jews who followed him. Let's think, then, of Abraham as the Old Testament model. What do we know of his personal spiritual pilgrimage?

When he was seventy-five years old, Abraham was told by God to leave the security of his home in Ur and move to the land of Canaan. There he spent the rest of his days in tents, never owning the land on which his flocks grazed. But God made him a promise concerning a people, a land, and a special seed.

In Genesis 12:2, God promised Abraham that he would be the father of Israel: "I will make you a great nation." God also promised Abraham that this people would own a specific piece of real estate: "All the land which you see, I will give it to you and to your descendants forever" (Gen. 13:15). Finally, God promised Abraham that through his line a Saviour would be born: "In your seed all the nations of the earth shall be blessed" (Gen. 22:18). These three declarations form the heart of the Old Testament covenant between God and His people.

How did Abraham respond to God's promises? The Scriptures are precise: "He believed in the Lord; and He [Jehovah] reckoned it to him as righteousness" (Gen. 15:6). Doesn't this verse remind you of Paul's description of what it means to believe in Christ? "But to the one who does not work, but believes in Him who justifies the ungodly, his faith is reckoned as righteousness" (Rom. 4:5). Both Abraham and Paul entered into eternal life by trusting in God. God has pledged Himself to declare righteous all who depend on His saving promise.

In the last chapter, we defined faith in three ways: personal choice, dependence, and a covenant relationship. Let's see how each aspect of saving faith is illustrated in Abraham's experience.

Faith involves a personal choice. I believe Abraham had a conversion experience. The language in Genesis 15:6 supports this. Abraham's determination to depend upon Jehovah as his God had a very decisive element to it, and God's response was equally decisive. In a split second, God imputed righteousness to Abraham; that is, righteousness he had not earned was ascribed to Abraham's account. His destiny was forever changed by this act of believing.

Faith involves dependence. When God told Abraham to sacrifice his son on Mount Moriah (Mount Zion), Abraham did so out of his complete dependence on God's integrity. God had previously told Abraham that He would establish His covenant through Isaac and his descendants. Because Abraham depended on this truth, he believed that either God would intervene (and spare Isaac's life) or He would raise Isaac from the dead! (Heb. 11:19) Note that Abraham's willingness to depend on God alone is tested through obedience. In the same way, James teaches us that people who really trust in Christ demonstrate their dependence upon Him by their desire to follow the Lord: "I will show you my faith by my works" (James 2:18). He also tells us that Abraham's "faith was working" when he offered up Isaac (2:21-22). Only because Abraham was depending on God's promise could he yield up his beloved son. Interestingly, James adds that in this act of obedience, "The Scripture was fulfilled which says, 'And Abraham believed God, and it was reckoned to him as righteousness'" (2:23). Thus, in all ages, people are saved by faith alone; but when God is believed and depended on, when our hope is transferred to the Lord, our conduct begins to change.

Faith involves a covenant relationship. Although we can speak of Abraham's faith as a crisis experience, such an understanding does an injustice to the full meaning of faith exercised by this man. God drew Abraham into a covenant agreement. The wording is very specific: "I will establish My covenant between Me and you . . . an everlasting covenant, to be God to you" (Gen. 17:7). This covenant arrangement meant that Abraham would acknowledge he was entering into a permanent arrangement with God on God's terms. What was the arrangement? Abraham would have a personal relationship with God Almighty! Central to this living relationship with God was the acknowledgment that Jehovah was Abraham's sovereign Lord. To make this point strikingly clear, Abraham and his descendants were to submit to circumcision (17:11). This dramatic sign would be a perpetual reminder to every Israelite that he was the Lord's.

Do you see the parallels between Old Testament faith and New Testament faith? In both periods, faith is central to God's dealings with humanity. We enter into saving faith by making a decisive personal choice because we are persuaded that God's promises are true. We choose to depend on Him alone as our saving hope. We acknowledge that we are totally incapable of saving ourselves. This saving choice involves the decision to enter into a personal covenant relationship with the living God on His terms.

The abundant life. The Old Testament primarily concerns itself with the quality of the earthly life of the people of Israel. The Old Testament is a blueprint for happiness for that special nation God raised up to be His own after bringing them out of Egypt. Their theocracy was totally unprecedented. Central to this theocracy was the responsibility to obey God's laws. Six hundred specific examples of "case law" expanded the meaning of the moral law of God (love God, love your neighbor) and regulated daily life in Israel. These laws were guideposts for abundant living. Indeed, the very word *Torah* connotes the idea of God pointing His finger, guiding us in the right direction. These laws made possible social freedom for people who would otherwise have been destroyed by each other's selfishness. God's laws liberate, but law keeping does not save us.

Some Christians think the Apostle Paul taught that at one time people were saved by keeping the Law and that Christ changed this. Actually, Paul taught that the Law was never given as a means of salvation. The Jews of Paul's day were using the Law in the wrong way, for to them it had become a way of salvation. Paul attacked this misuse of the Law rather than the Law itself.

God spoke through Moses: "All the commandments that I am commanding you today you shall be careful to do, that you may live" (Deut. 8:1). Some understand this to show that at one time God taught His people they could find salvation by keeping the Law. They further believe that God later changed His mind and announced a new hope—righteousness by faith. Thus, they conclude that the Old Testament message of salvation is qualitatively different from the New Testament message.

Moses was not, however, describing the way of salvation. He was telling his people that there was a way to live abundantly on earth. His speech in Deuteronomy was given just before Israel went into the promised land. Listen now to the entire quotation:

All the commandments that I am commanding you today you shall be careful to do, that you may live and multiply, and go in and possess the land which the Lord swore to give to your forefathers. (8:1)

Such teachings prescribed the way of blessing for the nation of Israel in space and time. Never do they describe the way of salvation!

I wish the way of salvation was defined more clearly in the Old Testament. I do not believe you can find a concise presentation of how to get to heaven anywhere in those thirty-nine books. God's saving plan was shadowy at best to the Old Testament saints.

Apparently, God had something else in mind when He revealed Himself through Old Testament law: He wanted us to know that He is holy and good. His precepts could be reduced to two supreme laws: *Love God,* and as an outgrowth of this divine relationship, *Love each other.* Isn't this exactly what Jesus Christ said? (See Matthew 22:36-40.)

The promise of God. What few salvation references we find in the Old Testament have two themes: atonement through blood and the certainty of a coming Messiah. Look diligently through the Old Testament and you will see this common thread, which we might call "the saving promises of God."

Prophets of old progressively revealed to the people of Israel that their eternal well-being was bound up in the coming of the Messiah. This great redemptive hope can be traced all the way back to Genesis 3:15. Here, in cryptic references, we meet Jesus Christ for the first time. He is described as one born of a woman who would ultimately conquer sin and Satan through a decisive battle. Satan would inflict a painful wound on the Son of God (Calvary), but the Messiah would prevail and inflict a fatal wound (resurrection) on His enemy. This, undoubtedly, is what Adam trusted in after he disobeyed God and found himself in need of a Saviour.

Another example of an Old Testament saint who lived by faith is Job. In many ways, his whole life was a test of his faith in a life beyond the grave. Job was once rich and successful. Then he became the object of Satan's taunts before God: "Job only serves you because of what he can get from you!" God responded by saying, "Let's find out." When Job was stripped of health, family, and possessions, what would he do?

Job became the object of close scrutiny as he faced a series of brutal personal tribulations. In the midst of it all, he said:

> As for me, I know that my Redeemer lives, and at the last He will take His stand on the earth. Even after my skin is flayed, yet without my flesh I shall see God. (Job 19:25-26)

Here was a man who was saved by his faith in a personal Redeemer. He had complete assurance that long after his flesh rotted in the ground, he would stand with his Lord in a resurrected body on the earth. Job apparently believed in promises God had personally revealed to him about resurrection life.

A thousand years later, King David greatly clarified the believer's hope of eternal life as he penned (by inspiration of the Holy Spirit) the beautiful words of Psalm 16:

> I have set the Lord continually before me; because He is at my right hand, I will not be shaken. Therefore my heart is glad, and my glory rejoices; my flesh also will dwell securely. For Thou wilt not abandon my soul to Sheol; neither wilt Thou allow Thy Holy One to see the pit. Thou wilt make known to me the path of life; in Thy presence is fullness of joy; in Thy right hand there are pleasures forever. (vv. 8-11)

What is David saying? He is describing how the "Holy One," the Messiah, will ultimately rise from the dead and establish His eternal kingdom. But he is saying more than this. He says specifically, "Thou wilt not abandon my soul to Sheol." David also had hope of resurrection! He was confident that because he was depending upon Jehovah, he would ultimately experience "pleasures forever" in God's heavenly presence.

The sacrificial system. Although salvation was by faith alone, the Jewish sacrificial system was still critically important to Israel's well-being. The Book of Leviticus describes a way for sinful people to be right and live in communion with God Almighty. It contains solemn and precise instructions for entering into God's presence. Blood sacrifices were essential to this process. As we read these instructions, we realize immediately that God was doing more than merely providing illustrations of salvation (or types) for the future church. God was not trifling here. Obedience led to life; disobedience, to death.

The Jewish sacrificial system confuses many Christians, but if we are going to be effective Gospel sharers, we must see the part it played in God's plan. A way to understand these sacrifices is to see them as fulfilling three purposes: *dedication*, reminding the people of Israel that they belonged to the Lord and lived in a special covenant relationship to Him; *expiation*, covering the sins of the people so that God could fellowship with them; and *celebration*, expressing the sincere thanksgiving of their hearts to God.

These sacrifices, though vitally important, did not take God's people to heaven. You will be hopelessly confused if you think for one moment that the Jewish sacrifices are the Old Testament doorway to eternal life. Through the sacrifices, Israel declared their loyalty to God, sins were covered and fellowship was restored, and they celebrated God's goodness on their behalf.

Above all, God established the sacrificial system to drive home the radical implications of His holiness. Blood sacrifices present us with a visual explanation of how sinful people can fellowship with a holy God.

Man in his sinfulness could not enter the holy place of the tabernacle. In order for him to come into the holy place, he had to be cleansed. This was accomplished through blood sacrifice. Do you see how this sacrificial framework was ultimately intended to prepare the Jewish nation for the all-sufficient sacrifice of Christ? Indeed, Christ's passion, His blood, His agonizing cross make absolutely no sense at all if they are not regarded by us as the divinely appointed, substitutionary means of our cleansing.

The animal sacrifices were necessary for the Jews to maintain their fellowship with God in this earthly life, but they were never to be seen as a ticket to heaven. From the beginning, the saints were saved through their faith in God's promise, just as we are.

The Gospel of the Kingdom During the Life of Christ

The day came when angels announced the birth of Christ. Suppose you were alive then: you walked with Him along Galilean roads and you enjoyed His teachings and His miracles. But before He was crucified, you died. You had not been privy to His secret instructions to His disciples in which He disclosed the manner and meaning of His death. You knew nothing about the cross. What would you have had to know about Him to have gone to heaven?

Many good people did die during that time. They could not possibly have known that Christ was soon to be crucified. Christ was probably recognized as Abraham's special seed and David's royal son in a unique sense, but could Christ's followers have anticipated the cross? I think not.

Christ preached a message that He called "the gospel of the kingdom." Matthew chronicles the beginning of Christ's public ministry by saying, "Jesus was going about in all Galilee, teaching in their synagogues, and proclaiming the gospel of the kingdom" (4:23). The gospel of the kingdom was the belief that peace would come to the world through the rule of the Messiah. It was enough for people alive at that time to believe that Christ was the promised Messiah. In accepting this truth and transferring their hope to Jesus Christ, they found peace with God.

Do you remember old Simeon? He looked at the baby Jesus when He was brought to the temple in Jerusalem and said, "Now Lord, Thou dost let Thy bond-servant depart in peace, according to Thy word; for mine eyes have seen Thy salvation" (Luke 2:29-30). Simeon died in peace because he believed this infant was God's Messiah. Christ had come!

Throughout His ministry, Jesus explained in more detail what it meant to live by faith. He often contrasted genuine faith with the artificial religion of the Pharisees of the time, as in the following story:

Two men went up into the temple to pray, one a Pharisee,

and the other a tax-gatherer. The Pharisee stood and was praying thus to himself, "God, I thank Thee that I am not like other people: swindlers, unjust, adulterers, or even like this tax-gatherer. I fast twice a week; I pay tithes of all that I get."

But the tax-gatherer, standing some distance away, was even unwilling to lift up his eyes to heaven, but was beating his breast, saying, "God be merciful to me, the sinner!"

I tell you, this man went down to his house justified rather than the other; for everyone who exalts himself shall be humbled, but he who humbles himself shall be exalted. (Luke 18:10-14)

The Pharisee had religion, but he lacked faith. The humble tax-gatherer's heart throbbed with personal conviction and guilt. As he pled for God's mercy, he was actually saying, "God be *mercy seated* to me so that You can righteously forgive my sin." He had in view the Old Testament picture of the holy God meeting sinners only on the basis of blood sprinkled on the mercy seat. This story concludes with Christ's assurance that "this man went down to his house justified." The Saviour thus described the nature of justification by faith—looking to God alone for mercy we don't deserve.

"The Messiah is here. He lives among us!" So heralded His first-century followers who believed the gospel of the kingdom. "He is the source of our deliverance!" All who depended on this truth found peace. As with believers of any age, God saw their faith and declared them to be righteous.

The Gospel of the Cross: God's Ultimate Revelation
The New Testament writers finish God's redemptive story in the Bible by declaring that those who embrace the "gospel of the grace of God" will see their lives transformed. They will know a degree of assurance never experienced before. They will no longer suffer from fuzzy thinking about how sinners can come to terms with a holy God. Consider with me how clearly the Apostle Paul declares the way of salvation.

The Book of Romans is not technically a Gospel, but nowhere in the Bible is the Gospel as clearly outlined. Theologians remind us that Paul had never been to Rome, so this book was his exhaustive explanation of the way of salvation to people he did not know. Thus, it cannot be ignored by those of us today who want to present the Gospel accurately.

Paul begins by declaring that a personal God exists who is characterized by righteousness (Rom. 1) and fairness (Rom. 2). Although God is the source of human life, the human race has rebelled shamelessly against Him. Gradually the lie develops that says, "We don't need a god! We can be completely fulfilled within ourselves." Having declared themselves autonomous, people feel free to pursue selfish appetites. Absorbed in the pursuit of gratification, they don't appreciate their descent into a pit of slavery to sin from which there is little hope of return.

Yet God revealed His grace to this pathetic humanity.

> But now apart from the Law the righteousness of God has been manifested, being witnessed by the Law and the Prophets, even the righteousness of God through faith in Jesus Christ for all those who believe; for there is no distinction; for all have sinned and fall short of the glory of God, being justified as a gift by His grace through the redemption which is in Christ Jesus; whom God displayed publicly as a propitiation in His blood through faith. This was to demonstrate His righteousness, because in the forbearance of God He passed over the sins previously committed; for the demonstration, I say, of His righteousness at the present time, that He might be just and the justifier of the one who has faith in Jesus. Where then is boasting? It is excluded. By what kind of law? Of works? No, but by a law of faith. For we maintain that a man is justified by faith apart from works of the Law. (Rom. 3:21-28)

My own pastor, Lance Latham, considered this passage to be the jewel of the Scriptures. In no other passage do we find the legal basis of our salvation. In no other place do we catch such a clear picture of the significance of the death of Jesus Christ.

The meaning of the cross for humanity. Paul declares that we are justified freely by God's grace through the redemptive work of Jesus Christ (Rom. 3:24). With these words, Paul explains how God's grace operates. God is able to justify the helpless because His salvation is without cost to the sinner. The key word is *redemption.* Simply defined, *redemption* means that all that was required to purchase our pardon from sin and find deliverance from its dominion over us was supplied by Jesus Christ. His sacrifice was sufficient.

Christ died because there was no other way to destroy sin's hold on us. The pathetic thing about religion is its arrogance. It claims to provide solutions. They never work. They lead ultimately to either hypocrisy or despair. Charles Dickens' Oliver Twist experienced both debtor's prison and the life of the petty thief before his wealthy grandfather rescued him. Oliver was free; he was rich, and he was loved! Such are the characteristics of all who have experienced the wonder of redemption.

The meaning of the cross for Almighty God. If Romans 3:24 gives us a human view of the cross, the next verse offers a Godward perspective. How does the cross affect God's thoughts and actions?

We answer this question in confessed humility, for "who has known the mind of the Lord?" (Rom. 11:34) Certainly there is mystery here. At the root of the matter is the word *propitiation,* which means a divine satisfaction. The perfect demands of God's unchanging holiness were completely satisfied by the blood sacrifice of Christ, and thus He could righteously offer pardon to sinners.

The question is often asked, "If God arbitrarily forgives sinners, doesn't He compromise His nature? If He winks at sin, doesn't He tarnish His holiness?" The answer to these questions is that God never winks at sin. It is always paid for in full. Not one sin will ever go unpunished. Christ paid for them all.

It was the Apostle Paul's mission to define for all time and for all people God's ultimate way of salvation. How thankful we can be that we have an objective Gospel. We can understand it; we can communicate it; we can be sure that it will never change.

Our New Relationship to the Old Testament

One reason Christians are confused about the way of salvation in the Old Testament is that they sense correctly that the church is not governed by the Law of Moses in the same way that Israel was. Paul tells us in Galatians 3:23-25 that we are not bound by the civil and ceremonial laws of the Old Testament. These verses may make you a little uncomfortable. They may cause you to ask, "Isn't God's Word eternally settled? How can we set aside God's Word?

An illustration has helped me see the answer to this question. When a young girl is growing up, she is under the authority of her father. She must honor and obey him. But when she gets married, she finds herself in a new relationship to her parents. She can still learn from her parents' counsel and profit from their wisdom, but she is no longer obligated to obey them.

Christians may understand the Old Testament Law in the same way. The word *Torah* means "finger pointing to God." The Law of Moses is a wise governess, lovingly pointing out the Father's will to the minor children.

But then Christ established His church out of people from many nations. Like the bride who has a new relationship to her father, the bride of Christ has a new relationship to the Law of Moses. Certainly, the Old and New Testaments are equally inspired. But God has found the ultimate means of showing us His ways. He has given us His Son! We still learn about God from the Old Covenant, but we are not bound by it. That is why we worship on Sunday rather than the Sabbath. That is why we don't offer animal sacrifices or travel to Jerusalem for the annual religious festivals.

Let the Old Testament be to you a finger pointing to God. Learn great lessons about God's ways from the Old Testament. But remember that the church of Jesus Christ enjoys a new relationship with God that is predicated upon the New Testament, the finished work of Christ, and the ministry of the Holy Spirit.

Know the Scriptures!

The confidence we need to share our faith must have deep roots. The only adequate source for this confidence is the Word of God. On a recent trip to Tanzania, I listened with fascination as a veteran missionary contrasted the saving message of the Scriptures with the teachings of the Koran. During his forty years of Muslim evangelism this man had been asked all the tough ones: How can God have a son? How can Christians say they worship one God when in fact they worship three? Why didn't Jesus know the hour of His return?

This man was undaunted by such questions because he knew the Scriptures. We must know them as well. We must particularly concentrate on the passages that speak to the four crucial issues of Christianity. There is so much material in the Bible about our need for God, the effects of sin, God's provision of Christ, and the nature of saving faith.

If you haven't got time for such an exhaustive study, at least review each Scripture reference in this chapter. You may want to underline them in your own Bible. Get comfortable with the way they read in the translation you prefer. You will feel more at home with some of these references than others; these you should consider memorizing.

You must understand that this is where your authority comes from. When you are prepared to set forth your case for Christianity by letting God's record speak for itself, you will discover that few people can intimidate you.

Thinking It Over

- What did Old Testament sinners need to do to be saved?
- What did people who lived and died while Christ conducted His earthly ministry have to know or do to be saved?
- How does the word *redemption* explain the meaning of Christ's crucifixion from a human perspective?
- How does the word *propitiation* explain the significance of the death of Christ from God's perspective?
- Is there more than one Gospel revealed in the Bible? Is there more than one way of obtaining eternal life?

CHAPTER 7
Justification and Faith

I am amazed that you are so quickly deserting Him who called you by the grace of Christ, for a different gospel. (Galatians 1:6)

One reason Christians do not feel more comfortable about their faith is that salvation is mysterious. Recently I talked to a pastor of a church who expressed his reservations about the theology of new birth. "Dick, if I preached that message, our people would spend their lives looking for illusive subjective experiences." He could not comprehend how people could have a solid basis for faith if it were divorced from something tangible like baptism. I tried to explain that the object of our saving faith is very tangible and completely objective: we put our faith in Christ; then God translates our faith into righteousness.

Some neighbors of ours are really into positive thinking. Basically, they believe you can have anything you want if you only believe hard enough. You may know people who think the same way. As pleasant as their words sound, they are deceiving themselves. Many sadly believe that by faith they can make what is imaginary real. The Scriptures teach no such thing. Rather, true faith makes the invisible real. God does not ask us to invent Christ, heaven, or the Holy Spirit by using our imaginations. These things are already real, but they are invisible. By faith, we accept their reality, and our lives are personally revolutionized.

Faith is useless unless it is placed in the proper object, so in order to share Christ effectively, we must be able to define quite precisely what it means to believe in Christ. We dare not be vague and careless about this life and death issue. Just what do we mean when we say that a person is justified by faith in Christ?

Because there is both urgency and mystery in this question, let's try to answer it in a systematic way. Perhaps one of the twentieth century's greatest minds can help our understanding. J. Gresham Machen has been called one of the most important American theologians of the first half of the twentieth century. When Dr. Machen saw his own denomination fall into the fashionable liberalism of the 1930s, he felt compelled to write about the biblical meaning of the Christian faith. His book *What Is Faith* (Macmillan) is an acknowledged classic. I want to share with you some quotations from Machen's book with the hope that they will help you explain to others what we mean when we say that we are justified by faith. Let's see if his insights can help remove some of the scales of confusion from our eyes.

Faith's Object: The Person and Work of Jesus Christ

The Apostle Paul told the Galatians that we are "justified in Christ" (2:17). In these three words, the Bible links the Christian to all that Christ is and all that He has done for us. We exercise saving faith as we come to terms personally with who Christ is and with what He did for us on the cross.

Have you noticed, however, that people today see Christ in different ways? Some see Him as a revolutionary, others as a humanitarian, and still others as a guru who dispenses sage advice. How can we be sure about Christ's identity? How does Jesus Christ make a difference in human history? Listen to Machen:

How is it that Christ touches our lives?

The answer which the Word of God gives to that question is perfectly specific and perfectly plain. Christ touches our lives, according to the New Testament, through the Cross. We deserved eternal death, in accordance with the curse of God's law; but the Lord Jesus, because He loved us, took upon Himself the guilt of our sins and died instead of us on Calvary. And faith consists simply in our acceptance of that wondrous gift. (p. 143)

I am simply amazed at how many people hold great respect for the person of Christ but have a very difficult time finding the assurance of personal salvation through Him. Recently, I had a conversation with a woman who said, "I have always known I was a sinner. I have always had reverence for the Lord Jesus Christ. My problem was that I had no satisfactory answer to the question 'Why should He save me?' It took years for me to see that my assurance must be rooted in His sacrifice for my sins at Calvary. When I finally understood that He died for me on the cross, I immediately opened my heart to Him and found the peace I so longed for."

Do you see the object of faith? We trust in Christ as Saviour and Lord, for He is the Lord Jesus Christ. Only because He is the Lord (God) is He able to pay the penalty for our sins (and be worthy of our devotion). Only because He is the Christ (the suffering Messiah) is He able to be approached by sinful people. We simply cannot separate who He is from what He did. Because He is Christ the Lord, Jesus is both the object of our worship and the object of our saving hope, and the Holy Spirit enables the seeker to believe both truths simultaneously.

Machen declares, "Christ touches our lives . . . through the Cross." Bask in this truth. The doorway into a personal relationship with the living God is the cross of Christ. Little wonder then that Paul said, "I determined to know nothing among you except Jesus Christ, and Him crucified" (1 Cor. 2:2).

In our day, some would make that door to be something other than the cross. Some insist on a charismatic experience and others insist on water baptism, but the mysterious secret that unlocks eternal life is so beautifully revealed by Machen: "He loved us . . . and died instead of us on Calvary. And faith consists in our acceptance of that wondrous gift."

Machen asserts that the primary task of every witness of Christ is to point our listeners to Christ's saving work:

> It is just the message about Jesus, the message that sets forth
> His cross and resurrection, that brings us into contact with
> Him. Without that message He would be forever remote—a
> great Person, but one with whom we could have no commu-
> nion—but through that message He comes to be our Saviour.
> True communion with Christ comes not when a man merely
> says, in contemplating the Cross, "This was a righteous man,"
> or "This was a son of God," but when he says with tears of
> gratitude and joy, "He loved me and gave Himself for me."
> There is a wonderful clause in the Westminster *Shorter
> Catechism* which puts the true state of the case in classic
> form. "Faith in Jesus Christ," says the Catechism, "is a saving
> grace, whereby we receive and rest upon Him alone for salva-
> tion, *as He is offered to us in the gospel.*" In that last clause,
> "as He is offered to us in the gospel," we have the centre and
> core of the whole matter. The Lord Jesus Christ does us no
> good, no matter how great He may be, unless He is offered to
> us; and as a matter of fact He is offered to us in the good news
> of His redeeming work. (pp. 151–152)

Faith's Strength: The Word of God

Not too long ago, I was enjoying a stimulating conversation with
a friend over lunch when my friend surprised me by asking,
"Pastor, how can I find the gift of faith?" At first, I thought his
question was a smoke screen. Gradually, I began to realize that
he was asking a very basic question. After all, does not history
record that many have declared themselves to be messiahs? Even
if we limit the messianic field to Christ alone, how can we be
sure that Christ's death really solves our problem? How can we
know with certainty that Jesus rose from the dead? Indeed, my
friend asked, "How can we be sure of anything with respect to a
man who lived two thousand years ago?" To such questions,
Machen speaks directly:

> We ought never, therefore, to set present communion with
> Christ, as so many are doing, in opposition to the gospel; we

ought never to say that we are interested in what Christ does for us now, but are not so much interested in what He did long ago. Do you know what soon happens when men talk in that way? The answer is only too plain. They soon lose all contact with the real Christ; what they call "Christ" in the soul soon comes to have little to do with the actual person, Jesus of Nazareth; their religion would really remain essentially the same if scientific history should prove that such a person as Jesus never lived. In other words, they soon came to substitute the imaginings of their own hearts for what God has revealed; they substitute mysticism for Christianity as the religion of their souls.

That danger should be avoided by the Christian man with all his might and main. God has given us an anchor for our souls; He has anchored us to Himself by the message of the Cross. Let us never cast that anchor off; let us never weaken our connection with the events upon which our faith is based. Such dependence upon the past will never prevent us from having present communion with Christ; our communion with Him will be as inward, as intimate, as untrammelled by any barriers of sense, as the communion of which the mystics boast; but unlike the communion of the mystics it will be communion not with the imaginings of our own hearts, but with the real Saviour Jesus Christ. The gospel of redemption through the Cross and resurrection of Christ is not a barrier between us and Christ, but it is the blessed tie, by which, with the cords of His love, He has bound us forever to Him. (pp. 153–154)

I do not believe you will ever succeed in sharing your faith if you lack confidence in the power of the Word of God to nurture faith in others. You must be persuaded that you have two powerful spiritual weapons at your disposal. You have the facts of history concerning Christ's life and you have a perfect record of those saving facts. We call this record the Bible. Don't ever underestimate the power of God's Word to persuade people!

Faith comes from hearing the Word of God (Rom. 10:17). Remember that "the word of God is living and active and sharper than any two-edged sword" and effectively penetrates the heart of the sinner (Heb. 4:12). Quite frankly, I do not know any fruitful evangelists who are not convinced that their success in persuading listeners to trust in Christ is rooted in the power of the Word of God.

Apart from this perfect record, those we seek to persuade may love the idea of Christ, but they will never be knocked off their feet by the reality of Christ. It takes the Scriptures to produce such conviction. Do you think the whole task of persuasion falls on your shoulders? It does not. Our part is to make others aware of the claims of Christ from the Scriptures themselves. The Spirit of God will do the rest!

Through the years, people have ignored my arguments, but when I quietly quote the Scriptures, reactions intensify. Some get quiet; others get hostile. No one can be neutral to something as powerful as the Word of God. Recently, representatives from the Gideons visited the University of Wisconsin in Madison. They distributed 12,000 New Testaments to students. During the Gideons' visit, they were harassed by a few who were almost possessed with the determination that these books must not get into students' hands. One young woman literally began tearing New Testaments apart with a fury that was quite supernatural. Satan hates that Book!

Do not depend on your debating skills to be persuasive. Depend rather on the truths concerning Jesus Christ that are simply stated in the Scriptures. Paul told Timothy that the Scriptures "are able to give you the wisdom that leads to salvation" (2 Tim. 3:15).

Faith's Confidence: He Gave Himself for Me

Recently, I met with a woman who told me that her faith was rooted in her childhood, but that most of her friends in her childhood church were not true believers, nor was the Gospel preached in clarity.

"How, then, did you come to faith?" I asked.

She smiled and said, "I'm not really sure. It wasn't through any special occasion. I just remember hearing my pastor explain to me that Christ died for my sins and rose again from the grave.

Something clicked in me. It was really quite simple. Yet as the years went by, I gradually saw that few others really believed what I did. I have no idea why these precious truths about Christ had such a life-changing effect on me when so many others who listened to the same facts remain unaffected."

Dr. Machen's words help us to understand what this young woman was trying to say.

> Acceptance of the Lord Jesus Christ, as He is offered to us in the gospel of His redeeming work, is saving faith. Despairing of any salvation to be obtained by our own efforts, we simply trust in Him to save us; we say no longer, as we contemplate the Cross, merely "He saved others" or "He saved the world" or "He saved the Church"; but we say, every one of us, by the strange individualizing power of faith, "He loved *me* and gave Himself for *me*." When a man once says that, in his heart and not merely with his lips, then no matter what his guilt may be, no matter how far he is beyond any human pale, no matter how little opportunity he has for making good the evil that he has done, he is a ransomed soul, a child of God forever. (p. 154)

The mystery element of Christianity is precisely that there is a "strange individualizing power" in faith. As I say this, I am tempted to suggest that the fatal flaw of some denominations is the ancient tradition of confirmation. Based on the polite nodding of the heads of this year's confirmation class (as the pastor recites the creeds), all eighth graders are confirmed in the faith! How careful we pastors must be not to create the impression that we superintend "soul factories" that crank out nothing but a superficially religious product each year at confirmation time.

Genuine faith is personal. It is the response of an *individual* to God's convicting Spirit. We must let God do His work of drawing people to Himself one at a time. Certainly, we must sensitively discern felt needs. We must know the Scriptures intimately. We must listen, share, respond, exhort, persuade, but we cannot turn on the light bulb. That is something only God can do. Watch for those bright eyes in your listener which so eloquently shout,

"Yes! I see it—I finally see it! He loved me and gave Himself for me!"

Faith's Counterpart: Mere Verbal Creeds

The great creedal affirmations that have codified Christian doctrine have had a beneficial effect on the church through the centuries. They have helped to bring continuity to the church's doctrinal position from generation to generation. But creeds can also be dangerous. Can you imagine how harmful they can become when mere verbal assent to their propositions is accepted by church leaders as an adequate demonstration of saving faith and sufficient grounds for church membership?

I am told that missionaries of the medieval church often made the mistake of equating some outward rite of the church with the mysterious saving work of the Holy Spirit. Francis Xavier is said to have baptized thousands in India. These thousands may have understood nothing of the regenerating work of the Spirit. Although they joined the church, many of them remained strangers to the new birth.

Dr. Machen saw this tragedy going on around him in some of the Presbyterian circles in which he moved. So stirred was he that he penned these words of warning:

> In order . . . that the purity of the Church may be preserved, a confession of faith in Christ must be required of all those who would become Church members. But what kind of confession must it be? I for my part think that it ought to be not merely a verbal confession, but a credible confession. One of the very greatest evils of present-day religious life, it seems to me, is the reception into the Church of persons who merely repeat a form of words such as "I accept Christ as my personal Saviour," without giving the slightest evidence to show that they know what such words mean. As a consequence of this practice, hosts of persons are being received into the Church on the basis, as has been well said, of nothing more than a vague admiration for the moral character of Jesus, or else on the basis of a vague purpose of engaging in humanitarian work. One such person within the Church does more harm to the

cause of Christ, I for my part believe, than ten such persons outside; and the whole practice ought to be radically changed. The truth is that the ecclesiastical currency in our day has been sadly debased; Church membership, as well as Church office, no longer means what it ought to mean. In view of such a situation, we ought, I think, to have reality at least; instead of comforting ourselves with columns of church statistics, we ought to face the facts; we ought to recall this paper currency and get back to a standard of gold.

To that end, it should, I think, be made much harder than it now is to enter the Church: the confession of faith that is required should be a credible confession; and if it becomes evident upon examination that a candidate has no notion of what he is doing, he should be advised to enter upon a course of instruction before he becomes a member of the Church. (pp. 155–157)

Certainly, by introducing the subject of church membership, Dr. Machen is addressing broader issues than we need resolve in our personal evangelism training. Yet I offer no apology in quoting these paragraphs. Human persuasion does not produce spiritual reality. By fleshly methods alone you may convince me to buy a vacuum cleaner that I do not want (I have always been a sucker for a good sales pitch!) but you cannot convert me to a Saviour I do not want! You cannot convert me to a Gospel that I do not understand; you cannot force my heart to repent; you cannot insist that I believe.

No wonder Peter cautions us to share the Gospel of Christ "in meekness and fear." Do you remember our definition of evangelism—sharing the good news of Christ in the power of the Holy Spirit and leaving the results to God?

When I was a young Christian in college, I was burdened to share my faith with someone I loved very much. As I approached his front door, I gritted my teeth with resolve, "I am not going to leave this place until my friend has made a decision!" Sure enough, a decision was made. Unfortunately, that convert was mine—not Christ's. The decision came from my pressure rather than from the Holy Spirit.

Faith's Result: God Alone Receives the Glory

When God's saving plan is obscured or twisted by earthbound thinking, you will sense it in the way people view salvation. God will be only two inches taller than us. Sinners will feel that they have the capacity to achieve their own salvation. The cross will be explained merely as a great demonstration of love (of which we are all capable). And of course God's grace will be rendered unnecessary.

May it never be!

The salvation offered in the Christian Gospel is vastly different. By the Spirit's power, two crucial transactions take place the moment we believe. The first is that we are justified. Our legal standing before God changes completely. Whereas once we were guilty and under God's wrath, we are now declared to be righteous. The divine records in heaven are altered forever. Our names are entered in the Book of Life. Never forget that we are declared righteous in God's sight because the very righteousness of Christ is imputed to us; that is, Christ's perfect righteousness is transferred to our account. Second, by His power we are regenerated. The Holy Spirit enables us to enter into the resurrection life of our Lord. Regeneration means that our inner selves come alive spiritually because the Holy Spirit takes up residence within us. *Regeneration* is the theological word that means "new birth."

Can you understand that when God saves us He changes both our legal standing before Him and our heart attitudes? He imputes righteousness to our heavenly bank account and He imparts to our souls a new desire to know Christ and serve Him. Salvation is all of God.

Why is it so important to God that we understand we are saved "by grace through faith"? Why is this unique message of justification by faith alone so nonnegotiable to God? Machen answers these questions masterfully:

The true reason why faith is given such an exclusive place by the New Testament, so far as the attainment of salvation is concerned . . . is that faith means receiving something, not doing something or even being something. To say, therefore, that our faith saves us means that we do not save ourselves even in slightest measure, but that God saves us. . . . The very centre and core of the whole Bible is the doctrine of the grace of God—the grace of God which depends not one whit upon anything that is in man, but is absolutely undeserved, resistless and sovereign. . . . The centre of the Bible, and the centre of Christianity, is found in the grace of God; and the necessary corollary of the grace of God is salvation through faith alone. (pp. 173–174)

We dare not take pride in our attainment of faith for we must see it as God's precious gift to us (Eph. 2:8). Let not our boast be in the attainment of faith, but rather, in the object of our faith— Jesus Christ our Lord.

What does this mean for evangelism? If salvation is of the Lord, is evangelism irrelevant? Is our responsibility to come to the moment of decision a deception? No, indeed. God is sovereign, and we are responsible. The Bible teaches both. God does not command you to understand this mystery, but He does ask you to accept it. This mystery adds to God's glory, for His ways are high above ours. Jesus' command is that I go into all the world with the Gospel (Matt. 28:19-20). This clearly is my part. But the Scriptures also teach that God is taking out from people on every continent "a people for His name" (Acts 15:14).

Practical Implications

In case you are wondering if systematic theology is practical, I would like to close this chapter by sharing an application for personal evangelism from each of the five aspects of saving faith.

Because faith's object is the Christ of the Bible, we must accept the exclusiveness of Christianity. The explosive implication of what we are sharing is that Christ is the only hope for us. As a consequence of this, every Christian must look on the Gospel message as the world's most precious resource. We must both guard it and share it. We must point people to the cross; we must explain the meaning of the tomb. Christians are bought by blood and owned by the risen Christ.

Because faith's strength is the Word of God, we must never underestimate the power of that Word. Soon you will share with a friend a compelling thought from the Scriptures that you have memorized. You will be amazed at how people respond to the Scriptures. It melts and it hardens. If you would witness with confidence, sharpen your weapons. Memorize key Scripture passages.

Because faith's confidence is personal assurance of salvation, we must never force people into a superficial decision. This will forever be the temptation of a zealous sharer. It must be our sincere aim to communicate the Gospel story with such emphasis on the love and grace of God (shown through the cross) that our listener sees through the eye of faith that Calvary covers all his or her sins and exclaims in breathless wonder, "He loves me and gave Himself for me!"

Because faith's counterfeit is a mere creedal profession, we must emphasize that salvation means knowing God. The cross is the doorway into a spiritual union with Jesus Christ. The Holy Spirit brings to us a longing for fellowship and communion with Jesus Christ. Regeneration (the Holy Spirit living within us and making us spiritually alive) is real.

Because faith's result is God's glorification, we must see ourselves as His instruments and ambassadors in a saving process that is much bigger than ourselves. My friend, you will panic and choke if you falsely assume that everything depends on you. As we mature in our ability to share Christ, we will sense His opportunities, His way of convicting of sin, His way of showing love, and His time for that precious moment of decision. Most importantly, we will give Him all the glory, rejoicing that He desires us to be part of the process.

Thinking It Over
- Why is it so important that salvation is through faith alone?
- How does salvation by grace through faith relate to the glory of God?

PART THREE

What Will It Take?

A
Method!

PROLOGUE TO PART THREE
CONFIDENCE COMES FROM HAVING A PLAN

Now that we understand the theology of the Gospel, we can pursue a workable methodology. Until we sense that we can be natural in witnessing, we simply won't do it. The sad truth is that most people have not found an approach to sharing Christ that makes them feel comfortable.

The next three chapters offer a methodology designed to meet this need. The approach depends on mastery of four crucial issues. These issues constitute the irreducible core of the Gospel. They focus on God, sin, Christ, and faith. When you know these issues, you know enough to lead a friend to Christ. Everything else is just putting meat on the skeleton.

Central to our approach is the idea of knowing God. Human frustrations can usually be traced to the fact that people live in quiet rebellion against God instead of in right relation to Him. Christ is the doorway to a personal relationship with the living God and the source of eternal life.

The point of entry into our Gospel presentation is the universal preoccupation with meaning in life. What must a person know or be to live with significance? Is there a secret to a fulfilling life? When our listeners truly identify with this question, they are well on the way to being won to Christ.

Each of the four crucial issues is rooted in important Scripture passages, and each concept is clearly defined. Central to this approach is a series of questions, so that your presentation is in the context of a true dialogue, not a monologue. The crucial issues, Scripture verses, definitions, and questions form the bulk of what should be committed to memory.

We offer no formulas, and there are no pat answers to be found here. We offer only a logical sequence of subjects that one must face before making an informed decision.

Make these your goals: to master the four crucial issues so effectively that you feel great liberty to improvise, to develop personal illustrations, to know at what speed to move ahead through the Gospel with different people. And practice! Share with believers and nonbelievers until you transform my methodology into yours!

CHAPTER 8
The Hurdles of Evangelistic Opportunity

But we proved to be gentle among you, as a nursing mother tenderly cares for her own children. Having thus a fond affection for you, we were well-pleased to impart to you not only the gospel of God but also our own lives, because you had become very dear to us. (1 Thessalonians 2:7-8)

Do you remember Edwin Moses? He is one of the finest athletes this country has ever produced. Unfortunately, his specialty is an athletic event you normally do not read about on the sports page of your local newspaper. Edwin Moses has given himself to an event that is virtually forgotten until it is time for that great quadrennial sports carnival we know as the Olympic Games.

The event is the 400-meter hurdles. Eight athletes dig in at the starting line. Between them and the finish line stand ten hurdle fences that require the athlete to leap thirty-six inches into the air at regular intervals. Speed, agility, concentration, and coordination are all needed to win. Moses has them all. He won the gold medal at the Montreal games in 1976. Eight years passed. Now he was warming up on a track in Los Angeles, California. Could he win again?

Hearts pounded as the starter's gun discharged. The result was never in doubt. With remarkable ease, Edwin Moses proved again that he was in a class by himself. As our national anthem was played in recognition of his feat, Moses' countenance clearly revealed that those years of practice and sacrifice were worth it all.

But whom do you know whose personal passion is the high hurdle event? For some reason, this strenuous event has no big following. So much is demanded of these athletes. They must be able to do more than sprint; they must be able to soar. People don't want to give themselves to this event because there are just too many ways to lose.

Is it possible that a parallel exists between this race and effective evangelism? In both fields, there are few who really commit themselves to intensive training and regular practice. In both spheres, participants tend to lose heart when they knock over a few hurdles. In both arenas, the discipline required to win may not seem worth the sacrifices. Soul-winning requires endurance and concentration. We are usually not successful in sharing our faith until a number of formidable obstacles are hurdled. Which of these hurdles has kept you from sharing your faith?

Hurdle One: You don't feel you know enough about the Bible to answer people's questions.

Hurdle Two: Your circle of friends is made up almost entirely of Christians.

Hurdle Three: Your testimony is not very unusual or interesting.

Hurdle Four: If you try to share Christ now, others will wonder why you waited so long.

Hurdle Five: You don't know if your friends are truly Christians or not.

Hurdle Six: You wish there was an easy way to get into the Gospel.

This would be a good time for you to pause for prayer. Pray that the following material will lead you to take concrete and specific steps to get over the hurdles that immobilize you.

Hurdle One: "I Have No Theological Training!"
Do you know someone who is consistently winning others to

Christ on a personal basis? Let me make a prediction. The one who just popped into your mind is probably not a seminary professor or even a pastor. Certainly, most pastors can give a public invitation, but I do not know of many pastors who are reaching out to neighbors.

Does it strike you as curious that these up-front people are not always the most successful in winning others to Christ? You might even discover that most of the personal evangelism you know about is being done by people who are still young in the Lord themselves. Bible knowledge and formal theological training are surely not detriments to personal evangelism.

Still, the question stands: why don't theologians make the best evangelists? Obviously, part of the answer revolves around spiritual gifts. The gift of teaching is distinct from the gift of evangelism. However, there just may be more to this question than giftedness.

Becky Pippert was in Madison recently conducting a seminar for about 400 people on the subject of evangelism as a lifestyle. She was amazing! It's impossible to get bored listening to Becky. When she finishes, you feel like saying, "More, Becky! Tell me more!"

When you stop to think about this woman's gift of communication, you realize that she shares stories with which all can identify. Before you know it, she has effortlessly brought you into her kitchen, her living room, and even into her prayer closet. When she is through, you don't feel preached at; instead, you feel as though you know her. And you know that her God is alive and her faith is working.

Becky said in effect, "Stop trying to talk like your pastor and start learning how to be yourself. Quit using cliches and tell people in simple words what it is like for you to know God." She challenged us by suggesting that if we were really serious about sharing Christ, we ought to develop three skills: ask questions, tell real-life stories about knowing God, and be with non-Christians in everyday situations over an extended period of time. God used this woman to challenge me.

Hurdle Helper: Be yourself. For evangelism to be successful, it must be natural. This naturalness, in turn, depends on our ability to flesh out a simple Gospel outline with timely insights from our own heart and personal experience. Do you see why it is so important for us to know Christ intimately, in such a way that we recognize His daily involvement in our lives?

We don't need formal theological training. We need daily to experience the presence of Christ. Why should anyone be interested in knowing *your* God? Are you finding Him to be a true source of daily deliverance and encouragement? Are you convinced by your own experience that life doesn't work apart from the Lord Jesus? Is He really this world's only hope? Do you believe that He alone can make people whole? If your answer to these questions is yes, you are on your way to becoming a relevant communicator of Gospel truth.

Hurdle Two: "I Have No Unbelieving Friends"

When I became a Christian during my teen years, I gradually experienced a change in relationships. Tom, Randy, and Dave were good buddies from the football team. We did crazy things together like knocking over all the garbage cans on the street and going skinny dipping in the neighborhood pool. But as time passed, my interests changed. By the time I enrolled in college, I found myself virtually cut off from the old guard.

It wasn't until years later that God impressed me with the importance of going out of my way to maintain a few special relationships with non-Christians. In Matthew Jesus is described as a "friend of tax-gatherers and sinners" (11:19). It occurred to me that Jesus Christ went out of His way to cultivate such relationships. Study the Gospels and you will be amazed at how many times the Lord won people to Himself before He won them for the kingdom.

People will always be drawn to thoughtful, cheerful, and giving people. Your neighbors are looking for friends who have the kind of personality traits that ought to be present in believers. Perhaps the reason more evangelicals don't have nonevangelical friends is that they don't take the time; it is just not important enough.

Harry Dickelman went home to be with the Lord several years ago. For years Harry pioneered the Lay Ministry of Campus Crusade for Christ. His home was always open to everyone. Harry was sometimes criticized for his approach (as pioneers usually are), but I will always treasure his memory, as he refused to allow his Christianity to create a social barrier between himself and others. Harry introduced more unchurched men and women to the Lord than anyone I know, because he enjoyed people for who they were.

Hurdle Helper: Cultivate friendships. Evangelism is a costly process. There can be but one response to the hurdle of having no unbelieving friends. Cultivate them. This will not happen accidentally. Decisions must be made. Whom will you ask over for dinner this month? Just friends from your church? Whom will you call? To whom will you demonstrate thoughtful kindness? We must learn not to blame those outside of Christ for our unfortunate alienation. We are the ones who have failed to take the initiative.

Today is a great day to get started! Talk over with your spouse or roommate how you can begin to take the friendship initiative. Such initiatives ought to be built right into your monthly schedule. This is the only way you will stay with it.

Hurdle Three: "I Don't Have a Testimony!"

Christianity is all about knowing God. Although almost everyone can talk about religion, few can talk comfortably about knowing God. Not only is there a world of difference between the two topics, but each produces a different effect on others.

Think of how many arguments you have heard about religion. Do you really think anyone profits from such confrontations? Now recall the last time a deeply spiritual friend shared with you how God was speaking to his heart or how the Lord Jesus had brought him through a personal trial. One kind of conversation repels; the other attracts.

The purpose of sharing your testimony is to whet your listener's spiritual appetite. ("Hey, she has really found something wonderful that I don't have!") Everyone who wants to be used in evangelism ought to give careful attention to the question, "How did I come to place my faith in Christ?"

Often in an evangelism training workshop, someone will say,

"But I don't have a testimony!" Some feel that because they trusted in Christ at an early age their spiritual stories are boring. Others are confused about when they put their faith in Christ (some of you have walked down the aisle twelve times!).

Hurdle Helper: Your personal testimony can be exciting. Whether you came to Christ as a child or an octogenarian, in tears or matter-of-factly, in a decisive moment or through a stormy process, your testimony can be exciting. You are a living example of how God can change a human life.

What makes a testimony exciting? It is not necessarily the particular process God uses. Rather it is the fact of finding a cure to the human predicament of being trapped by sin and alienated from God. Last week a young man came into my office and said that through prayer God had healed a deformed leg. I find such accounts tremendously exciting! If you understand what I am saying, you will see why the testimony of one converted at age six is just as exciting as that of a Hollywood movie star.

There are six components of an effective testimony. Let's examine two different kinds of testimonies.

The Historical Testimony

The historical testimony traces through time the events that led to conversion and should include these six vital components.

1. *Life without Christ can't satisfy completely.* Whatever I was and had and did before I put my trust in Christ simply wasn't enough. Remember, the enemy has been seducing people with one basic lie from the beginning of human history: "You will be happier if you live independently of God."

We begin with this thought because millions of people are pretending to be happy and fulfilled because they think others are. People are likely to identify with your candid admission that you discovered life wasn't all you had hoped it would be. We want to say something with which a non-Christian will identify personally. Never begin by saying, "Before I got saved . . . " Avoid cliches and irrelevant details.

Examples:

All of my childhood was spent dreaming of being the world's

greatest wrestler. I won the gold medal at the U.S. championship games, but as the medal was placed around my neck, I remember wondering, *Is this all there is to life?*

Ever since I can remember, I wanted to be an actress. It took years before I realized I was on a dead-end street.

I thought I had it made. Parties, girls, popularity, pot. My life had a lot of gusto—but something was missing.

I grew up in a wonderful home, but I had a real childhood fear. I went to my grandmother's funeral: they put her in a box and covered her with dirt. I didn't want that to happen to me!

2. *Religion can't solve the problem.* We must make a distinction between religion and Christianity, between liturgy and life in Christ. Religion is a human system. Salvation is supernatural. The sad thing about church is that it can become a substitute for Christ rather than a beacon pointing to Christ. Unhappy people usually turn to religion at some time in their lives. Generally it doesn't satisfy.

We don't seek to put down any denomination. Rather we want to emphasize that institutions cannot do for a hurting soul what Christ alone can do.

Examples:

For forty years I attended church regularly. Somehow I thought that God would accept me if I just came to church often enough.

During my high school days, my interest in church disappeared. I had to choose between parties and church—and I chose parties! Church just didn't mean anything to me.

I went to church to find release from my guilt and tension. All I found inside the church was a heavier burden. I would leave the service feeling worse than when I went in.

3. *Someone shared Christ with me.* Although reading a Bible all by yourself could do the trick, it doesn't usually happen that way. Christians almost always bridge the gap between the unbeliever and the saving message.

Think about it. How did you hear about Christ? You probably met someone who was unique both in message and in lifestyle. What did she or he say to you? Why did you take him or her seriously?

Examples:

I was invited to attend a special praise meeting that met in the basement of our church. The church was very liturgical, so I wasn't really prepared for what happened that night. But it was really wonderful! The main event of the evening was listening to a couple describe how Jesus Christ was changing their marriage now that they had put their trust in Him. I had never heard anything like this before!

I went to a church social with some friends. The next day their youth pastor came over and asked me if I wanted to go out for a Coke . . .

4. *At a point in time, I put my trust in Christ.* Some think of their conversion as a process. From our standpoint this is undoubtedly true. Few are converted the first time they hear the Gospel. But no matter how vague the process seems to us, we must believe the Scriptures, which teach that there is a moment in time when God declares us "not guilty."

Two questions may help you clarify this point in time. Was there a *circumstantial* crisis that helped you see your spiritual need? Was there an *intellectual* crisis that prompted your understanding of and reliance upon Christ's redemptive work? It is at this point in your testimony that you should mention sin, Christ's saving death, and how you put your faith in Him.

Example:

I really had a chip on my shoulder. I had made a subconscious decision to live only for myself. I didn't mind using people to get what I wanted. That all changed when I attended a Campus Life meeting. Somebody shared that Christ loved us so much that He gave His life on the cross for us. She said that if we would trust in Him, we could know real peace—both with God and with ourselves. I think I had been waiting for this message all my life. I received Jesus Christ as my own personal Saviour that night.

5. *Though I'm not perfect, I'm different now.* Don't allow your listener to get the wrong idea. Explain that becoming a Christian does not solve all problems, eliminate all pressures, or obliterate all psychological and physical deficiencies. Christians aren't perfect—only forgiven. We can still sin. But Christians do have peace, because we are not in rebellion against God anymore. We have joy, because we know that we are His children. We have new attitudes, because the Holy Spirit indwells us and enables us to be Christlike in our character. But Christian character is a progressive thing.

Examples:
When I first heard about Jesus Christ, I thought that if I became a Christian, pressures at the office would disappear. You know what happened? When I was converted, the pressure increased! But that's not all; Jesus gave me a growing capacity to handle it.

I trusted Christ twenty-five years ago. You would think that by now I would have perfected the Christian life, wouldn't you? But I'm still learning, still growing, still fighting. I still battle against sin, but that's part of God's plan. Happiness comes from saying no to sin each day. The Holy Spirit gives me the power to do this.

6. *Now I have peace with God.* Many are religious. Few have peace with God. Many go to church and know the creeds. Few know for sure that their sins are forgiven. Therefore, no testimony is complete until we have communicated that faith in Christ has resulted in the assurance of salvation. Every Christian has the

right to say, "I'm a child of God—a citizen of heaven!" Others take note of those who have a humble and quiet confidence that their sins are forgiven and that they are possessors of life eternal.

Examples:
You know, it's kind of hard to explain. But since Christ has come into my life, I have real peace with God. I'm forgiven. God is now my Father!

I've now walked with the Lord for twenty-five years. Never once in all of that time have I ever doubted that if I were to die, I would go immediately into heaven to be with the Lord. Death holds no fears for me.

The Philosophical Testimony

The philosophical testimony traces the thought process that led to conversion through a logical sequence. The philosophic testimony has the advantage of being able to integrate a significant Gospel presentation with one's own intellectual quest for meaning. Your testimony is the account of how you came to terms with four troublesome issues. We'll follow a single testimony through each of these four issues.

1. *Why am I here?* This is the question of meaning.

When I came to the University of Wisconsin three years ago, I was really geared up for a good time! True to my impulses, I gave myself to the pursuit of pleasure. For the first year of my college life, I don't believe there was a weekend when I didn't attend a party. Somehow, no matter how drunk I got, I always managed to find my way home.

Gradually, I found myself being victimized by the law of diminishing returns. As much as I tried to fight it, I heard a voice deep within saying, "There is no ultimate satisfaction in what you are doing." Almost in spite of myself, I began to wonder why I was alive. Was there any meaning to my life?

One day while having lunch at the Student Union, I overheard a conversation between two students. One was trying to persuade the other that there was a personal God behind all of creation. Apart from that belief, life could not make any ultimate sense. I was amused by this young "evangelist."

But in the coming weeks, I found myself haunted by the idea of God. Gradually, I came to see that the student was right—life's secret is God. If there is a God, and if He created every individual in a unique way, then there must be a purpose for each one of our lives.

2. *What is wrong with me?* This is the question of failure.

To know that there is a God in heaven is one thing. How to explain why a creature of His feels as empty as I did is quite another. I will never forget how God showed me the answer. One night there was a knock at the door of my dorm room. Amazingly, the fellow I had seen at the Union now stood at my door! He invited me to come to a Bible study in our dorm. For the next eight weeks, we met together on Tuesday evenings, and for the first time I learned some of the things the Bible has to say. The most important thing I learned was an explanation for this emptiness I felt. The Bible says that our sinfulness keeps us from knowing God. Sin is basically a deep-seated, selfish instinct that says, "I am going to have my own way." It is found in everybody, and apart from God's help, there is no cure for it.

Now, for the bad news. I learned that sin has serious consequences. It not only cuts us off from God, but it cuts us off from each other and even from ourselves. No wonder so many people are saying, "I wish I could get my act together!"

3. *Who can help me?* This is the question of a deliverer.

The fellow who was leading the Bible study invited me to go out with him for a pizza. We started talking. Actually, he started talking. He got a bright look in his eyes and then started telling me about Jesus Christ. He told me that Jesus Christ truly was the Son of God who came into this world, not only to show us what God is like, but to die for our sins on the cross. He showed me two statements that Jesus made when He was dying that really startled me. When Jesus said, "My God, My God, why have You forsaken Me?" He was aware of the fact that His Heavenly Father had turned His back on Him because He literally had become our sin bearer and God, in His holiness, can't look at sin.

But then my friend showed me the verse in the Scripture where Christ cried out from the cross, "It is finished!" He didn't say, "I am finished." He said, "It is finished." That means Christ succeeded in His mission.

4. *How do I relate to Christ?* This is the question of response.

After my friend described in vivid detail the crucifixion of Christ, he shook me up by asking a question. He said, "Why do so many people say they believe in Jesus Christ, but still don't have peace with God?" I had no answer—I don't think he expected one. He began to explain that there is a difference between what most people think of as faith and what the Bible says about faith. People equate faith with knowledge, but the Bible teaches that faith is more than that. Faith is the personal choice to depend on the fact that Jesus Christ, the Son of God, died for my sins. If the Bible is right, every person must come to a moment of decision. That night sitting in a restaurant with my friend Dave I came to that moment of decision. I placed my faith in Jesus Christ as *my* Lord and Saviour.

Hurdle Four: "I've Been Silent with Friends Too Long!"
There are always some who insist that they find it more difficult to share Christ with friends than with strangers. Such persons are inhibited by thinking, "What will she think of me if I share Christ with her now? After all, we've been working together for three years. I should have integrated my faith into our conversations a long time ago. Now, I feel trapped into remaining silent!"

Hurdle Helper: Building bridges into the question of life's meaning. The following paragraphs are designed to help you visualize ways in which you can comfortably begin a spiritual conversation with people you have known for a long time. What we must do is construct conversational bridges that are kind, sincere, and straightforward attempts to introduce the subject of meaning or purpose in life.

The church bridge:
You're right, John. I am excited about our church. I think it's because we are scratching where people itch. Our pastor has been teaching us that the purpose of our church is to point people in our community to a meaningful and fulfilling life in this world and to eternal life in the next.

My life hasn't always been real fulfilling, but some things have really changed in my world since I started to sort out my spiritual concerns. What about you, John? What comes to mind when you ask yourself if your life has any ultimate significance?

The personal experience bridge:
Sue, do you realize that we have both been working at this bank for two years now? We have talked together about so many things; yet there is an important part of my life I have never shared with you. Can I tell you how I got a handle on the scary question of the meaning of life?

The philosophy bridge:
Kevin, we have been friends for years and we have done a lot of crazy things together. We have talked about almost everything under the sun. But there is a subject of growing interest to me that I don't think we have ever discussed. Do you mind if I ask you a rather philosophical question? Where are you in your own personal search for meaning?

The current issues bridge:
Yes, Joan, the arms race does seem to be out of control. The more I think about nuclear missiles, the more I wonder what is ahead for the human race. What about you? Does the thought of nuclear war ever make you wonder about the meaning of life? How do you cope with your fears about the future?

The loneliness bridge:

Yes, Beth, I sometimes feel lonely, but not nearly as much as I used to. I came to the point in my own loneliness where I questioned whether or not I would be missed if I died. It was a tough time. I had to ask myself if I thought my life had any ultimate meaning. I'm glad now that I asked the question. Here is what I discovered.

The love bridge:

Marty, I really appreciate the confidence you have shown in me by telling me that you feel very unloved. Everybody needs to feel loved. When we cry out for love, we are saying that we want others to acknowledge that our lives have value. Do you think your life is significant?

From any of these bridges, it is a relatively easy procedure to move into the Gospel, as we shall demonstrate shortly.

Hurdle Five: "I Can't Tell Where Others Are Spiritually"

The Lord Jesus warns us about judging others (Matt. 7:1-2). It is so easy to come up with false conclusions about where people are spiritually when we base these conclusions on superficial criteria, such as smoking or drinking or attending a certain kind of church.

We must humbly confess that we are not very good at looking into the souls of others. We will be wiser if we permit people to speak for themselves, but people are conditioned to be tight-lipped about their attitudes toward spiritual things. They will probably not volunteer their views unless they are asked to do so.

Hurdle Helper: Three questions of spiritual discernment. The following questions have been used thousands of times to help friends clarify where they stand spiritually. Why not memorize them and ask them sincerely when you are given freedom to do so by the Holy Spirit?

Introductory question: Jim, where are you in your own search for meaning in life?

General question: Have you come to the place in your own

spiritual life where you know for sure that if you died today you would go to heaven?

Specific question: Suppose you were to die today and stand before the Lord and He should say, "Jim, why should I let you into My heaven?" What would your answer be?

The first question is really a conversation starter. Listen carefully to your listener's answer and ask the Lord to guide you into a conversation in which you can ask the general question. Although this general question is explosive, it can be answered with a simple yes or no. Because you are merely trying to discern a person's need at this point, move quickly from his answer to the general question into the specific question. This question probably reveals where your listener is really placing his hope of heaven. It is important that you repeat his answer to him. Clarify issues as much as you can. Later, after you have shared the Gospel, some people will try to convince you that they have always believed what you are saying. Then, you must remind them of how they responded to the question:

> Jim, do you remember when I asked you about what you would say if God asked you why He should let you into heaven? I've learned that although people sometimes think they believe in Christ, they usually reveal what they are really trusting in by the answer they give to this question.

Don't feel duty bound to ask any of these questions. If your listener is quite candid about his or her religious beliefs, you may find it unnecessary to pursue this sequence of thought altogether. It is up to you to decide whether these questions are appropriate in each witnessing situation.

Hurdle Six: "I Don't Know How to Get into the Gospel"
This may be the most formidable hurdle standing in your path. Many lose the race because they trip right here. One way to jump this hurdle is to simply introduce an outline as in the Campus Crusade question, "Have you heard of the four spiritual laws?" Simple approaches like this have helped millions to be fruitful sharers, but there is always a risk of seeming to be sharing

an outline rather than a heart concern. How can we get into the Gospel without running this risk?

Hurdle Helper: A secret that unfolds life's meaning. All of our conversation bridges in hurdle five introduced the question of life's ultimate meaning. It is in response to this question that we must be able to state comfortably, "Jim, the question of meaning began to come into focus when I discovered through reading the Bible that life has a secret. May I share that secret with you?"

Hurdle Helper: An open-ended question. If you enjoy being straightforward and creative, you might begin an evangelistic conversation like this: "Will you give me your reaction to this proposition: Each of us was born with a need to know God?"

Thinking It Over

- Which of the hurdles do you find to be the most difficult to jump over?
- What is a "purpose bridge"? How can you link your church's purpose to the question of meaning in life?
- What six components should be included in every testimony?
- What questions can help us understand where others are spiritually?

CHAPTER 9
Knowing God: A Fresh Approach to the Gospel

And he shall speak words to you by which you will be saved.
(Acts 11:14)

Conceptually, I have been writing this chapter for fifteen years. Literally, I have written and rewritten it three times. I have always felt that the results were inadequate. The problem: how do you teach evangelism without becoming either trite and simplistic or complex and overwhelming?

A year ago, I tried again. When I had finished, I had written a dialogue that looked like a Hollywood script. It was twenty pages of a hypothetical "here's what evangelism looks like" encounter with a fictitious acquaintance. Everything I sought to emphasize was included in it. When I put my pen down, I thought, "Maybe this is it!" But then came the test. When I tried to teach the chapter to our people, they became politely withdrawn.

Gradually, they built up the courage to pop my balloon and bring me back to reality. "This chapter is fine for you. It just won't work for me. Your thought patterns are different from mine. If sharing my faith depends on learning these twenty pages, God must be calling me to some other ministry!" I was crushed, but not for long.

One morning I went out for breakfast and on top of the menu was the heading Build a Breakfast. For a nominal price, one could order breakfast entrees to his liking: one juice, one fruit, one egg dish, one bread, one breakfast meat, and one beverage. I had a great breakfast that day, but more importantly I got an idea for presenting the Gospel. Wouldn't it be great if everyone could develop his or her own pattern of sharing Christ by selecting relevant ideas from five different kinds of evangelistic information? Here are the five areas:

1. Proclamation—declaring clearly the Good News of Christ
2. Interaction—learning how to ask relevant questions
3. Explanation—clarifying confusing or controversial concepts
4. Illustration—enabling the listener to identify with the truths shared
5. Objection—developing skills in responding to frequently asked questions

Now that you know the plan, open your menu. It's time to "build a conversation" that is both true to the Gospel and true to your own personality and experience.

Proclamation

Proclamation describes the task of declaring clearly the saving message of the Gospel. In chapter 5 I introduced the four crucial issues. These are simple assertions that declare that God has revealed a way people can know Him. Think of knowing God as the essence of salvation. Think of knowing God as the common denominator that integrates into a logical whole the four crucial issues of the Gospel. Here once again are the *four crucial issues.**

1. God: We have a need to know God.
2. Sin: Sin keeps us from knowing God.
3. Christ: Christ was crucified to solve our sin problem.
4. Faith: We can now know God by depending on Christ.

This is our message in its most basic form. Reduce it further and you destroy it. We should look at these facts as the skeleton

---

*For a handy, pocket-sized booklet entitled "Life's Toughest Question" summarizing the four crucial issues, write the author at Encounter Publications, 6101 University Ave., Madison, WI 53705.

of our witness.

How can we introduce them? Each of these issues could be introduced by tying them into a numerical outline, such as, "The first crucial issue concerns God," and so on. But when a numerical outline is used, you run the risk of sounding as if you have memorized a formula. Instead, I recommend the following logical outline:

1. Life has a secret: God
2. Mankind has a problem: Sin
3. God has a solution: Christ crucified
4. You have a responsibility: Faith

How can we state them clearly? These brief introductory sentences prepare the way for sharing the four crucial issues as clear and concise propositions. Notice that there are no difficult words or theological jargon in the way we state these truths.

1. God: Each of us was created with a need to know God.
2. Sin: Our sinfulness keeps us from knowing God.
3. Christ: God loved us enough to send His Son, Jesus Christ, to die on the cross to pay for our sins.
4. Faith: You can come to know God personally by placing your trust in Jesus Christ as your Saviour and Lord.

How can we substantiate them from the Scriptures? The Scripture verses you will want to use are both relevant and brief. Sometimes the verse supports the whole proposition and at other times it only supports one aspect of it.

1. God: "This is eternal life, that they may know Thee, the only true God" (John 17:3).
2. Sin: "Your iniquities [sins] have made a separation between you and your God" (Isa. 59:2).
3. Christ: We share two of Christ's words from the cross that explain His death—*forsaken*, the word of substitution (Matt. 26:46), and *finished*, the word of completion (John 19:30).
4. Faith: "God has given us eternal life and this life is in His Son. He who has the Son has the life" (1 John 5:11-12).

Each of these Scripture verses is fundamental to your presentation. Learn these core verses perfectly. Be sure you know the specific truth that each one substantiates. Then, memorize other verses to help you give a fuller explanation.

How can we clarify their meaning? There are really only two aspects of each crucial issue that you must master to clarify the Gospel.

1. God: Knowing God is life's secret. Knowing God is eternal life.

2. Sin: It's an attitude of rebellion. It's like an incurable disease.

3. Christ: He cried "forsaken" because He died to suffer the consequences for our sins. He cried "It is finished!" because He paid for our sins in full.

4. Faith: Faith is rooted in history yet goes beyond mere facts. Faith involves a decision.

Interaction

Let's turn our Gospel presentation into a dialogue. Sometimes less experienced evangelists are more comfortable when they do all the talking, but good communicators are good listeners. People like to know that you're interested in their point of view. Have you discovered that it can be a little tricky to have a positive dialogue about spiritual things? Either the religious zealot does all the talking or the discussion turns into a heated debate.

To avoid these extremes, we need to learn how to ask the right questions and listen carefully to the answers. Questions are the bridge between proclamation and explanation. After stating the Gospel proposition, we must determine which aspect of the truth shared needs further clarification.

A question about God. After declaring that we are born with a need to know God, you must acknowledge that not everyone chooses to enter into a relationship with Him. Ask a question like, "What happens when people deny their need to know God?" This question can lead to a discussion of the human predicament that is explained in the first chapter of Romans.

A question about sin. I have attempted to ask a question that is intended to be a bridge between an abstract, theological definition of sin and the felt needs of the listener. That question is, "How does sin affect our daily lives?" Unbelievably, few people make any correlation at all between sin and its everyday consequences. One thing is certain—before we look for a deliverer

AN OUTLINE OF THE EVANGELISM ENCOUNTER PRESENTATION OF THE GOSPEL

Life's toughest question: Does my life have any ultimate meaning?
Here's how I came to terms with this question:

My life started to make sense when I learned that...
1. Life has a secret: Each of us was born with a need to know God.
   A. Knowing God is life's secret.
   B. Knowing God is eternal life.

But obviously many people feel cut off from God. Why?
2. Mankind has a problem: Our sinfulness keeps us from knowing God.
   A. Sin is an attitude of rebellion.
   B. Sin is like an incurable disease.

It looks hopeless, but now God Himself enters the picture...
3. God has a solution: God loved us enough to send His Son, Jesus Christ, to die on the cross to pay for our sins.
   A. Christ cried, "Forsaken!" because He died suffering the consequences of our sins.
   B. Christ cried, "Finished!" because He paid for our sins in full.

But deliverance from sin doesn't come automatically...
4. Now you have a responsibility: You can come to know God personally by placing your trust in Jesus Christ as your Saviour and Lord.
   A. Faith in Christ is rooted in history.
   B. Faith in Christ involves a decision.

from sin, we must be able to appreciate how devastating sin is.

A question about the cross. The question related to Christ's crucifixion is intended to bring us from the first century to the twentieth century. Two thousand years ago, Christ died as our substitute and paid our debt in full. But what are the implications of the cross today? To span twenty centuries, we want to ask the question, "What does the cross mean to us now in the twentieth century?"

By asking this question, we gain the opportunity to clarify the twin themes of God's love and God's grace. The cross is your guarantee that God loves you! Every evangelist must develop a means of underscoring this theme, for there is power here. The knowledge of God's love for us has been the catalyst responsible for millions of conversions.

But the question arises, "How can sinners become right with God?" The stage is now set for a careful explanation of the meaning of saving faith.

A question about faith. Faith—God-given faith—will always have a quality of mystery to it. Why is it easy for some to believe? What about others, who say they would sell their most treasured possessions if only they could be granted faith? The Bible tells us that faith is a gift from God (Eph. 2:8), but it is also our responsibility (John 1:12). To complicate the picture even more, coming to faith is a real crisis event for some; others insist that their spiritual pilgrimage was a lengthy process.

The problem is that most people who have grown up in the United States think they have faith. How can we help our listeners to know the difference between faith that is mere mental assent and life-changing faith, planted in our hearts by God? The following question may be of some help: "Why do so many people who say they believe in Christ feel so unsure about their relationship with God?"

This question acknowledges that many people who think they believe lack true assurance of their salvation. Personally, I do not think many people really take time to analyze their religious experience.

"Faith" is often actually vague, wishful thinking on their part. Having asked many people this question about faith, I always marvel at the responses given. One such response is, "You know, I've wondered that myself!"

By asking this question, we are asking our listener to think through the faith question in a way he or she may never have done before. As we shall see in the next chapter, this question opens the door to the moment of decision.

Explanation

Explanation means that we must be able to defend our faith, relate it to life, clarify areas of confusion, and fight for a meeting of the minds. By asking the right questions, we discover what aspects of the Gospel need more explanation.

Through the years, I have discovered that each of the four crucial issues raises a major area of confusion.

Let's imagine how we might help people through this confusion using a hypothetical dialogue.

● When told that people need to know God, some ask, "Why do so many people deny this need? What happens when they do?"

"Beth, suppose we are born with a need to know God. What happens to human beings who ignore the fundamental needs of their lives? For example, what happens to people who refuse to eat?"

"They die."

"You're right. And a person who denies that he has a need to know God dies spiritually. What I mean by this is that without God, human life has no ultimate meaning. The Bible speaks directly to this issue. It describes the 'human predicament' like this: People are born with a need to know God. Because they would rather 'do their own thing' they suppress this inner, spiritual need. The Bible says: 'Professing themselves to be wise, they became foolish.' That is, they smugly told themselves that they didn't need any religious crutches to make life work. In effect, they exchanged faith in God for faith in man (Rom. 1:33-34).

"What happens when man becomes the measure of all things? Let me share with you some of the consequences of denying our need of God. First, without God, there is no higher law on which to base our own laws. Therefore, all human laws and values become arbitrary. Second, when societies come into a conflict of values, brute force alone determines who is right. Third, when life on earth is no longer seen as a stewardship from God, people live for personal gratification, pleasure, and power. To put it differently, they can find no compelling reason not to give in to their selfish desires. You see, with no ultimate accountability, human selfishness prevails.

"Just look at America today. As we became more and more of a secular society—as young people are told in schools and universities that there is no God—drug and alcohol abuse rages out of control, crime skyrockets, broken homes abound ... all because everyone is doing what is right in their own eyes.

"If this is true, why, then, would anyone deny his need of God? The answer to this important question has to do with a fatal flaw in human nature that the Bible calls ... sin."

● When told that sin is serious, some ask, "If sin is such a problem, how does it affect me?"

"Tim, when I look around, I see lots of unhappy people. Many are escaping from reality through the abuse of drugs, sex, and alcohol. Why? I think it's because people are experiencing just what the Bible says will happen when people sin. It warns that 'the wages of sin is death.' That means the consequence of our sin is always some form of alienation.

"When someone says, 'I wish I could get my act together,' he is really confessing that he is experiencing one form of this alienation. Sin cuts us off from ourselves. I think of this fact every time I hear someone moan about feeling incomplete, empty, meaningless. And I hear more and more people admit these feelings every day.

"There is another way sin may be affecting our society. Maybe you have heard some say, 'I wish I didn't feel so alone!' Now another dimension of the problem of alienation caused by our sinfulness is being felt. It is terrible to feel unloved, but sin makes people little islands of self-interest. We feel like others aren't really concerned about us and, to be honest, we wonder if we care about anybody else either.

"Sin also makes us a little ambivalent about God. On the one hand we say, 'I wish I could know God!' but on the other hand, we are afraid to find Him. It is part of our nature to want to run and hide when we have broken God's laws, and sometimes we wonder if sin makes God want to hide His face from us. The Bible warns us that those who reject God will be separated from

Him through all eternity.

"Do you understand what I am saying, Tim? Sin is a catastrophe! It cuts us off from a holy God, from others, and even from ourselves."

● When told that Christ is God's answer, some say, "I have always believed in God, but I thought you had to be good to get to heaven."

"Jenny, I am glad it excites you to know that God loved you enough to send His Son to the cross to die for you. Christ's death is a revelation of God's love for us.

"But it is more than that. The cross is God's way of telling us that eternal life (or the forgiveness of sins) can't be earned. When I was a boy, I thought the role of the church was to help everyone practice the Golden Rule. I thought we were all basically pretty good people, and the preacher's job was to remind us of our goodness.

"How wrong I was! I came to my senses by thinking about the cross. Yes, it does remind us that God loves us. But its real message is that our sin problem is so serious and our 'heart problem' so incurable that God in His perfect wisdom found only one way to cure us. His only Son, Jesus Christ, must die as our substitute, taking upon Himself the full penalty of sin that we deserve.

"Certainly, some people find this message distasteful because they desperately want to believe they have the capacity to save themselves. You see, good works are the human way to get to heaven. However, it is crushing when we realize that we can do nothing to solve our own sin problem.

"Christ's finished work is God's way to heaven. This path is the way of grace—a very important word in Christianity. First, grace means we must come to God in our weakness. (That's difficult for proud people to do!) Second, we find all that we need in Christ. God graciously offers to exchange our sin for Christ's righteousness. Wouldn't you think people would flock to God's grace? Well, they don't because grace is such a blow to their pride. To receive God's grace, we must come to Him as we are—helpless, guilty people who admit that we have no other hope. All we can do is lift empty hands toward heaven and tell God that we really do want deliverance from our sins and are ready to put our trust in His Son as our Saviour.

● When told that each person faces the task to believe, some ask, "How do I turn my knowledge about Christ into faith?"

"Why do so many people who say they believe in Christ feel so unsure about their relationship with God?"

"Maybe it is because people have a hard time explaining what it means to believe."

"You're right, Terry. Believing does mean different things to different people. By far, the most common view of faith is that it means we know something about God. In other words, faith means knowledge. Because most of us have had some religious education as children and have heard about Jesus Christ all our lives, it is easy for us to conclude that we are 'believers.'

"However, in the Bible, faith means dependence or, more specifically, the decision to transfer our dependence to Christ alone as the source of our deliverance from sin. Abraham Lincoln was a great president. Every American believes in him historically, but we don't believe *on* him. That is, we don't depend on him as the hope of our salvation. Faith in Christ is different. We can only become Christians as we choose to depend *on* Christ.

"Specifically, we must believe that Jesus Christ is truly God. If He were not truly God, His sacrifice on the cross could not pay for our sins. Clearly, the Bible declares that He is God. If you don't believe this, do a study of who is worthy of receiving worship according to the Bible. You will find that it is God alone. Yet, Christ receives the worship of people and angels. In fact, the angels of heaven are commanded to worship Him. The Bible says, 'Let all the angels of God worship Him!'

"We must also believe that Jesus Christ died for our sins. When a person really believes this, his whole life changes. For the first time, he believes there is a way of escape from this incurable condition. Here's a verse, 1 Peter 3:18, that says it all: 'For Christ died for sins once for all, the righteous for the unrighteous, to bring you to God.' The central pillar of Christianity is that God the Father is able to offer eternal life to us freely because of the perfect sacrifice of Jesus Christ.

"Saving faith is more than saying yes to a creed about Christ. He did not stay dead! He rose bodily from the grave to be the living Lord over His church. We exercise faith in Him by entering into a covenant relationship with Him as our Saviour, our Deliverer, our Lord, our God. Does the resurrection of Christ make sense to you? By it, we are convinced that Christ was no imposter. Because of it, we enter into a relationship with Christ as our living Lord."

The three areas of proclamation, interaction, and explanation are the primary building blocks of an adequate Gospel presentation. Still, you will be even better equipped to share Christ if you develop skills in two additional areas—illustration and answering objections.

Illustration

In an earlier chapter, I suggested that storytellers make good evangelists. Becky Pippert is a superb storyteller. Do you remember Ralph Merritt, the plumber? You've never heard such interesting tales! Storytellers have an uncanny ability to make you identify with what they are saying. When we share Christ, we must face the possibility that some will find it hard to identify with us. For this reason, we do well to develop graphic illustrations of the main truths we want to communicate. The following examples are not intended to be a complete arsenal of compelling illustrations, but I hope they will make you see the value of using illustrations and prompt you to start looking for your own.

Illustration about life's secret. Many consider St. Augustine to be the most brilliant scholar in the history of the Christian church. Not so well known, however, is that Augustine's early life was a headlong leap into debauchery and destructive passions. After seeing and doing it all, Augustine came to a profound conclusion that changed the very course of his life. He said, "Thou hast made us for Thyself and our souls are restless until they find their rest in Thee, O God!" Augustine finally entered into that rest. He discovered life's secret!

Illustration about humanity's problem. Do you remember the recent football strike? It was really kind of crazy! Players whose salaries averaged $350,000 annually and owners who have made fortunes in various business pursuits all decided they wanted a bigger piece of the pie. To me, the football strike was just one more example of human selfishness, which is the root of our sin problem. We all want our own way! Wars are fought because power-hungry politicians want their own way. Teachers and students fight in classrooms because they want their own way. I see it in every two-year-old. Behind those piercing stares is a little mind thinking, "I'm going to get what I want, and no one is going to stop me!" Because sin infects us all, it is not stretching the point to say that we all act a little like two-year-olds when we don't get what we want.

Illustrations about God's solution. Recently, I heard a story on the radio about a concerned father who wanted his son to understand the meaning of the cross. The father had warned the boy that if he came home late for dinner, he would have to pay the consequences. Sure enough, the son came home long after the agreed-upon hour. The conversation went something like this: "Son, do you know the hour?"

"Yes, Father."

"Do you remember the penalty?"

"Yes, Father: no supper and off to my room. But, Dad, can't you just forget about it this once?"

"No, Son, for then you will be late again." As they bowed their heads and said grace, the son heard a slight shuffle. When he opened his eyes, a big plate of food was set before him. In front of his father, there was an empty plate. Suddenly, the father left the table with these words, "Son, I love you but the penalty must be paid. I am going to my room. I will pay it for you." The son was never late again!

During the Civil War, a man who did not want to go to war could pay another man to take his place in the ranks. This man then entered the army in the name of his wealthy benefactor. Imagine a soldier, with your serial number, fighting your battle! Imagine further that you bought a local newspaper and read that a man with your name had been killed in combat. You suddenly realize that you are alive because another man took your place in death! *That* is what Jesus Christ did for us.

A mother was taking a walk in the woods with her two teen-age daughters. Everything was delightful until a bee landed on the arm of one of the girls. The girl let out a dreadful scream as the bee stung her. Just then, the bee took off and began to hover over the younger sister. The mother saw the look of terror in her pretty blue eyes. She quietly said, "Honey, don't be afraid. All of that bee's sting has already been spent on your sister. You have nothing to fear." In the same way, Christ has taken the sting out of death for us by dying in our place.

Illustrations about our responsibility. Carol and I love to window shop. What would happen if we came to a store with this sign in the window: EVERYTHING IN THE STORE IS FREE TODAY! The first thing we would do is laugh. What a clever way to capture people's attention! But then we would wonder. Is it possible? Everything depends on the integrity of the person who put up the sign. Can he or she be trusted? Let's see what happens when people go in. Sure enough, one person says, "Hey, I know the guy who owns this store. I am going in!" In five minutes, he comes out with armloads of high-class merchandise. All of a sudden, I am alone. Carol has just made a beeline through the doors. She sees the sign. She believes in the integrity of the one who wrote it. She sees the satisfying results of those who have gone in before her. Isn't Christianity like this? We hear the Gospel. We conclude that God is telling us the truth. We make our choice and enter in through the door—Jesus Christ.

Faith is similar to sitting down in a great big easy chair at the end of the day. The chair is well built so I know it will support me. All I have to do is collapse into its comfort. In the same way, God makes a promise to us. "I offer you eternal life and the forgiveness of sins through Jesus Christ. I offer it to you freely because My Son paid for it in full on the cross." What does God ask of us? To recline in His promise. We are to depend on—find rest in—what God has said and done for us.

Answering Objections

Many would-be evangelists remain on the sidelines because they secretly believe they witness from logical weakness while their listeners argue back from philosophical strength. Nothing could be farther from the truth. You will be helped in your witness if you keep two facts in mind: no one knows very much about ultimate realities, and it is always easier to ask a religious question than it is to answer one. We make a mistake by thinking that people have their philosophical house in tidy order. Few people really have a consistent worldview with regard to spiritual things. How can we use this awareness to our advantage? Let me offer one suggestion: learn to answer a difficult question by asking a question.

Recently, I squirmed as a timid evangelical was harangued by a salivating atheist on a television talk show. A pattern was established early in the program. The atheist asked the tough questions and the evangelical did his best to answer them. "What kind of God would create a world like this? Why does God allow people to be hungry? Why have so many atrocities been justified in the name of religion? Why can't denominations get together? Why are Christians so intolerant?" And so on.

The entire dialogue would have been different if the evangelical had asked a few questions in reply.

Atheist: What kind of God would create a world like this?

Christian: Which world are you talking about?

Atheist: Why this one, of course. This world in which there is so much pain, so much economic injustice, so much confusion. Does this world really seem like the best that a powerful God could do?

Christian: But what if this isn't the world that God created?

Atheist: Don't be silly. This is the only world we can talk about.

Christian: Not necessarily. What if God created a perfect world and then put people in the center of it, giving to them the capacity to choose their destiny? What if they chose to live in rebellion against God? Isn't it a human axiom that when people make selfish choices, others suffer?

Or take, for example, the questions that are so often raised about the Bible. It is time we overcame our defensiveness in standing for its accuracy. After all, when the authority question is raised, what options do people have?

Skeptic: Do you really believe in the Bible? How simplistic!

Christian: No, how wise! Where do you look for truth?

Skeptic: In science, of course.

Christian: How many times have scientific theories changed in the last two hundred years?

Skeptic: Many times. We are finding new data every day!

Christian: Doesn't it make more sense to look for truth in a source that never goes out of date? that has not been proven to be erroneous in over two thousand years? that gives people workable guidelines for happy living? that holds families together? that has never known its prophecies to fail? What truth source has a better track record?

I hope you are excited about the legitimacy of asking questions. You may find roles reversing. Your confidence may grow while the other person may become slightly less cocky. Still, no amount of question asking can absolve us from the responsibility to answer some questions. Here are some frequently presented objections.

How can anyone ever be sure about his knowledge of God? If God is personal, wouldn't you expect Him to be able to find a way to reveal Himself to us? If our eternal well-being depends on such a revelation, wouldn't you expect God to be able to set His truth source apart from all false ones in such a way that sincere seekers could know the difference? God's clearest expressions of truth come to us through Christ (the living Word) and the Bible (the written Word). To demonstrate the trustworthiness of Christ, God raised Him from the dead. To prove the reliability of the Scriptures, God gave the human authors a supernatural credential—the ability to perform convincing miracles. Additionally, the Holy Spirit confirms to our hearts that what the Bible says is true. If you are concerned about the issue of religious knowledge, let me suggest an experiment. Read through the Gospel of John carefully. After you are finished, see if your skepticism about God's ability to reveal Himself has changed.

Why do you insist that people cannot solve their own sin problem? The Prophet Jeremiah said it would be easier for an Ethiopian to change his skin or a leopard to change his spots than it would be for a sinner to cure himself of his sin (Jer.

13:23). Sin is not just something we do; it is something we are. Sin is a heart condition. You don't cure a heart condition by taking a shower. It is only by becoming spiritually alive through Christ that we find power over sin. Have you noticed that sin is not just a matter of knowing what is right or wrong? Criminals behind bars know they have broken laws. The real issue is finding the power and the desire to overcome the sin nature we possess. It can only be done through the power of the risen Christ.

How could God condemn people who never heard about Christ? This is an important question and a difficult one. It would be easy for me to switch roles with God and tell Him what is right and what is wrong, what He can do and what He can't. I would like to tell Him that He shouldn't banish anyone from His presence who has never heard the Gospel.

But the question that haunts me is this: How do I know that God will save anybody? By what means will any individual find deliverance? The answer I come up with is faith in Christ. "There is salvation in no one else; for there is no other name under heaven that has been given among men, by which we must be saved" (Acts 4:12).

The early Jewish believers in Christ were persecuted because they would not look at Christianity as just another sect of Judaism. Because they were convinced that Christ offered sinners their only hope of deliverance, they were martyred. The early church was persecuted because they preached an exclusive message. It is possible that God can reveal Christ to people in remote places through direct angelic or spiritual communication, but we do not know that He does. What we do know is that if our deliverance comes only through faith in Christ crucified, then every Christian on earth must spread the Good News.

It doesn't matter what you believe as long as you are sincere. I think this is wishful thinking. Many experiences teach us that sincerity alone is not always adequate. Millions of people sincerely believed that Hitler would not start a war. One of my favorite old ballplayers, Ernie Banks, always sincerely believed that the Cubs were going to win the World Series. They never did!

A hunter followed the tracks of a large deer through the snow one frosty morning. He was doing fine until he saw that the tracks crossed a frozen river. The ice looked thin, but he believed the ice would support him. When he gets to the middle of the river, will it be his sincerity or the thickness of the ice that matters?

A French general said, "Facts care little about how they are received by men. Though some embrace them and others reject them, they nevertheless remain facts." You must face God on His terms because you are dealing with truth, not opinion.

If God is all-powerful, why is there so much pain and suffering in His world? Evil and suffering in this world have been caused by the wrong choices people have made. God is not the author of suffering; man is. Whenever human beings choose to sin, someone gets hurt; someone suffers. Indeed, many suffer.

When Christ died on the cross at Calvary, He did so as part of the solution to the problem of evil. How unfortunate that people blame God for the problem of evil, when He has already given His only Son to solve the problem!

Let me list some further objections you may be confronted with as you share Christ. If one of them troubles you, do some homework until you have some idea of how to respond.

- I don't believe in miracles. This is the twentieth century, after all!
- Isn't the Bible just another "holy book" full of errors and personal biases?
- Most of the "born again" people I know have psychological problems!
- How do you know that your conversion experience wasn't just psychological?
- Won't a good moral life get me into heaven?

Don't let these objections overwhelm you. Think them through. Study the Scriptures. Why not develop a list of questions to ask others? Start with these:

- Do you ever ask yourself the question, "What if there is life after death?"
- Why haven't a thousand generations of humanity been able to transform this planet into a utopian garden?

- How do you explain the built-in sense of right and wrong in people?
- What do you think of Jesus Christ? What is your explanation of why His tomb was empty?
- Do you believe that your life has a satisfying, ultimate purpose?

The material presented in this chapter is extensive enough to overwhelm some who read it. Remember the task: build yourself a way of sharing your faith.

Start with a clear understanding of the big picture. Just what is the Gospel? It is Good News about how we can know God. Dwell on this basic idea; use it as the point of integration for everything you share.

Dwell on the four words of the Gospel—*God, sin, cross,* and *faith*. Do you understand them? Do they represent for you a logical sequence of thought? How will you introduce them? state them? substantiate them? clarify them?

After proclaiming the truths of the Gospel in a positive, sincere way, invite questions. This will help you know what aspects of each truth need further clarification and promote a more comfortable dialogue.

As part of the clarifying (explanation) process, strive to help your listener identify with the truths you are sharing. Finally, be kind to a person who objects to things you are saying. You are sharing important matters of the heart. The Holy Spirit is convicting. Don't be surprised if your listener gets a little defensive. Be patient. Win him or her with the soundness of your truth and the sincerity of your concern.

Thinking It Over
- What do you find most helpful about this Gospel presentation?
- What is the purpose of the interactive questions?
- What is the advantage of linking the consequences of sin to popular felt needs in our society?
- What two statements of Christ from the cross are central to our Gospel presentation? Why?
- What are some differences between the world's view of sin and that of the Christian?

CHAPTER 10
Approaching the Moment of Decision

For the Scripture says, "Whoever believes in him will not be disappointed." For there is no distinction between Jew and Greek; for the same Lord is Lord of all, abounding in riches for all who call upon Him; for "Whoever will call upon the name of the Lord will be saved." (Romans 10:11-13)

Tying the evangelistic knot can be an unsettling experience. During a recent Evangelism Encounter seminar an attractive young woman volunteered to take part in some role playing in front of the class. She was intellectually sharp, and we could tell right away that she had done her homework in mastering the four crucial issues.

As we had agreed, the young man interacting with her would periodically raise an objection. He was quite humorous in his attempt to play the role of a skeptical graduate student. With skill and finesse, she answered each question. By this time, the whole class was impressed with the presentation.

The student gradually warmed up to the Gospel. There was a basic agreement about the person and work of Christ. The moment of decision had arrived. Suddenly, this woman began to lose her composure. Her sense of assurance evaporated. She stammered through a mechanical decision process, but was completely unconvincing.

What had happened? Quite clearly, she was trying to express thoughts and ideas that were not really her own. In her mind, she was still profoundly confused about the whole idea of choosing to trust in Christ. She was no longer on comfortable ground.

She is not alone. I have listened to others say they become a little paranoid when they try to pull in the net. They think to themselves, *Am I going too fast or too slow? Am I making it too simple or too complicated? Is God convicting or am I manipulating?* Consumed by such fears, it is not hard to understand why Christians retreat to the sidelines of evangelism.

To bring a sense of order to the decision process, we must consider four questions: What is "a decision for Christ"? What are the logical steps that lead to the moment of decision? What constitutes the decision itself? How does one gain a solid sense of assurance?

What Is a Decision for Christ?
There is nothing magical or mysterious about a decision for Christ. We can understand it as simply the human means of exercising saving faith. Think of it as that moment in which a person who understands the facts of Christianity embraces them in his heart (by an act of the will) by choosing to depend on Christ alone as Saviour. Thus, this decision is made at the very second he exercises saving faith. Now it will be helpful to review what we learned about saving faith in Chapter 5.

The faith that produces eternal life has three parts. First, there must be a *choosing*. No one enters the kingdom by accident. No one will wake up in heaven, wipe the sleep from his eyes, and say, "Oh no! I didn't want to come here!" Paul wrote to the Romans, "With the heart man believes, resulting in righteousness" (10:10).

Second, there must be a *depending*. What we are asking for is nothing less than a transfer of trust. We exercise faith by transferring our hope of heaven from ourselves and our good deeds to Christ and His all-sufficient sacrifice for sin. The bottom line of faith is always revealed by asking the question, "What am I really depending on to save me?" The answer must be, "The saving work of Christ alone."

Third, there must be a *relating.* It is vitally important to help others understand that by exercising faith they are entering into a personal relationship with the risen Christ. God created Adam for fellowship, but sin destroyed that relationship. For thousands of years men have fought to live completely independent of God. We enter into salvation when we can again share God's life.

The symbolism of a bride and groom helps my understanding. Paul tells us that the church enjoys a relationship with Christ similar to the relationship a woman enjoys with her fiancé. They get to know each other; they learn what each offers the other; they contemplate the advantages of sharing a life together. One day, before family and friends, they say yes to each other and enter into a lifelong covenant relationship.

When we place our trust in Jesus Christ, we acknowledge Him to be our sovereign God and enter into a covenant relationship with Him based on this acknowledgment. This is not salvation by works. Rather it is a profound coming to terms with who Jesus Christ really is.

The Bible reveals that the early saints made their decisions in a variety of ways. There is no one right method. Whether a decision involves responding to questions, praying a prayer, or raising a hand, we must humbly acknowledge that these are only human devices to help people come to terms personally with who Christ is and with what He did.

Even with the decision process, we cannot always know when a person passes from death to life. Was Paul converted on the Damascus Road, or later when Ananias said to him, "Receive your sight"? (Acts 9:17-18) What kind of decision did Cornelius make? Luke states that he simply listened to Peter's proclamation of the Gospel and suddenly the Holy Spirit came upon him (Acts 10:44). Nobody extended an altar call to him!

If such diversity frustrates you, remember these insights. *Don't presume to limit God.* The saving power of God will always transcend our methodologies. This is where your sensitivity to the Holy Spirit comes in. Our part is to share the Gospel, explain the meaning of faith, help our listener place his trust in Christ, and let God do the rest.

Don't expect bells to ring! Often a person will not experience lasting assurance at the time of decision. But that is God's business. Learn to take people at their word and assume that God is working in their lives. Help them get off to a good start. It may take months or years before they grasp the full significance of what they have done.

Remember that this decision is not the pursuit of an emotional high but a reasonable response to truth. Do not encourage your friend to look for the "new birth," or she or he will conclude that salvation is an experience. Don't confuse the human role in salvation with God's role. God asks people only to believe. When people place their faith in Christ, God sends the Holy Spirit to regenerate them and make them spiritually alive.

Steps That Lead to the Moment of Decision

Let's now think through the issues that we must share as we explain the importance of making a decision for Christ.

1. ASK A QUESTION:
   Why do so many people say they believe in Jesus Christ, yet have no peace with God?
2. OFFER AN EXPLANATION:
   Biblical faith is more than knowledge. It is the personal choice to depend on Christ.
3. GIVE AN ILLUSTRATION:
   God wants to give you the gift of life, but it only becomes yours when you choose to accept it.
4. STATE YOUR EMPHASIS:
   You won't accept it until you are convinced you need it. You must want deliverance from sin and its consequences. You must want to know God and must realize this is only possible by trusting in His Son as your Saviour.
5. ASK ANOTHER QUESTION:
   Is there anything preventing you from putting your trust in Jesus Christ right now?

The moment of decision is an awesome moment. Somehow, through simple, inadequate words, a supernatural transaction takes place. I don't claim to understand the mysteries involved, but I believe the Apostle Paul, who told the Corinthians that through his words the Holy Spirit was writing on human hearts (2 Cor. 3:3).

You might want to preface your questions of decision like this:

A decision for Christ is really not such a scary thing. We simply take the facts we know are true in our heads and choose to rely on them from our hearts. The heart is really our inner control center, where choices are made. Now it is time for you to make your choice about Christ. Perhaps the best way to make this decision is simply to respond truthfully to three questions. May I help you make this decision by asking them of you?

The Question of Repentance:
Do you understand that you have a sin problem you cannot solve by yourself? Do you really want Christ to deliver you from your sin?

The Question of Recognition:
Now that you have admitted the problem, let's be sure you understand God's solution. Do you recognize that Jesus Christ died on the cross to pay for your sins?

The Question of Response:
All along I have been stressing that saving faith is the choice we make to rely upon Christ. Do you right now place your trust in Jesus Christ alone as your Saviour and Lord?

Gaining a Solid Sense of Assurance
By guiding an individual through the decision process, we are not only signaling that faith is an active thing, we are also declaring that faith commences at a moment in time. We may never be sure of the precise moment. Of one thing I am certain—many of us were not converted the first time we expressed an outward decision to accept Christ as Saviour. Don't let this discourage you, though. Be encouraged by remembering that the decision is only a vehicle for expressing total dependence upon Christ. Make trusting Christ—not the decision—your emphasis.

How do we then help a person who makes a decision gain solid assurance of his new life? It is time to turn to the record of Scripture. The Bible can be thought of as a valid courtroom document describing what has actually taken place. The Bible confirms reality to our hearts. If you have not yet opened a Bible in the course of your discussion, this would be a good time to open it together. Ask your friend to read 1 John 5:13 out loud several times. Then say something like this:

> You have just read a very powerful verse. If I understand it correctly, it was written to help us develop confidence and assurance about our new life in Christ. The writer was the Apostle John. He wrote this letter with one primary thought in mind: followers of Christ can *know* they are in a right relationship with God. We can take God at His word!

Getting Started in the Christian Life

Babies don't usually take very good care of themselves. They need to depend on their parents. In the same way, newborn Christians will flounder if left to themselves. All new believers need the kind of guidance and encouragement usually referred to as follow-up. Here are a few goals to keep in mind as you help your new brother or sister get off to a good start.

Immediate follow-up. The goal of immediate follow-up is to help the new believer understand the implications of new life in Christ. Read 2 Corinthians 5:17: "If any man is in Christ, he is a new creature." Discuss the blessings and positive implications of being new (e.g., a clean slate, a new outlook). Discuss the dangers of being a new baby (e.g., not knowing how to feed oneself, walk, or face danger).

It is also a good idea to stress that your friend did not become a Christian through any certain prayer or religious rite (such as baptism). As a believer, however, he or she will be greatly blessed by expressing thankfulness to God in prayer. Be sure to encourage a simple prayer from the heart. You can help your friend conceptualize the prayer, but don't ask him or her to pray after you.

New life in Christ is your focus for discussion. Take some time to discuss two questions to help a new believer understand that his new life carries with it certain implications. These questions are, How will I announce that I have new life in Christ? How will I nourish and protect it? I hope you can appreciate how important these questions are. The new believer has come to a crossroads in life: Will he or she be able to appreciate and accept the fact that something fundamental has changed?

Short-term follow-up. The goal of short-term follow-up is exposure to the Word, so now it is time to use your creative imagination. What means of short-term exposure to Scripture is this person most likely to appreciate? Would she or he be interested in a one-on-one study of the Gospel of John with you? Are you participating in a relevant small-group study that she might enjoy? Do you know of any special-interest group studies with which he would happily identify? (If she is a dentist, do you know of a Bible study made up of evangelical dentists?)

Long-range follow-up. The goal of long-range follow-up is personal commitment to a fellowship of believers. The implications of the Great Commission must not be ignored in the evangelism process. We have no right to consider the work of evangelism complete until a new believer has been brought into fellowship with a visible body of believers and has made a commitment to them. Christians must recognize that God does not want them to retreat into a comfortable refuge of self-interest. Christ calls us to exercise our gifts in the context of a local church. We need to hurt for others, laugh with others, and pray for others.

I hope you worship in a church that is vital and winsome. May it be the kind of place that makes it easy to accomplish these follow-up objectives.

Thinking It Over
- How do you know that believing the Gospel involves a moment of personal decision?
- What are the three components of faith?
- What is the only solid basis for assurance of salvation?
- Why ought you to go through the assurance issue before you ask your listener to say a prayer?

PART FOUR

What Will It Take?

A
Manifestation!

PROLOGUE TO PART FOUR
THE BODY RELATING IN LOVE: GOD'S CONVINCING MANIFESTATION

One of the city of Madison's claims to fame is its arboretum, home to one of the most breathtaking collections of lilacs to be found. With the arrival of the first week in May, my wife and I make our annual visit to smell the lilacs.

About a mile away from the arboretum, we start to smell the lilacs. By the time we reach the lilac grove, we fight for control—such fragrances! The colors—whites, blues, pinks, and purples—are a symphony of sight, but it is the smell that overcomes us. The routine of breathing becomes an act of worship. The fragrance of one bush may be ignored, but the aroma of many is irresistible.

Of course, there is a moral to this story. Christianity is being ignored. Too often people sniff a little around us and conclude, "No help here." The fragrance of one life is not always convincing. But when the saints gather together, what kind of aroma do they give off?

When we say only a few special people are called to do evangelism, we display thinking that is not only naively deficient but also dangerous. Isolate the lilacs and you dilute the manifestation. Search your Bible for any hint that evangelism was an individualistic endeavor. On the contrary, Luke in Acts describes it as a by-product of believers relating together.

The great first-century mood was one of anticipation: God will manifest Himself; the Holy Spirit will move among us; Christ will soon return. Sensing that their lives were a sham if they refused to open their hearts to God's will, the fragrance of Christ burst forth out of their brokenness.

Far too little has been written about the compelling role that the corporate manifestation of the Holy Spirit plays when a whole society is penetrated with the Gospel. The following chapters are my attempt to redress that oversight.

CHAPTER 11
The Pursuit of God in the Pursuit of Souls

This is the word of the Lord to Zerubbabel saying, "Not by might nor by power, but by My Spirit," says the Lord of hosts. (Zechariah 4:6)

Evangelism isn't a particularly new challenge. One of the most effective evangelists of all time lived more than 2,500 years ago. God called this man to preach to a city notorious for its brutality and wickedness. The man refused to go, but God would not be thwarted. He engineered a historic chain of events that ultimately sent such profound shock waves of evangelistic revival through the ancient city of Nineveh that the ultimate course of world history was altered.

Certainly, you must have wondered about Jonah's ministry to Nineveh. This unassuming prophet walked into the heart of the capital of the Assyrian empire, a city so vast that it took three days to walk around it (Jonah 3:3). The man of God told no jokes, presented no chalk talks. He had no P.A. system. No soothing organ strains prepared hearts for the invitation.

Yet his "crusade" boggles my mind. The Scriptures waste no words in chronicling the event. This is all we read: "Then Jonah . . . cried out and said, 'Yet forty days and Nineveh will be overthrown.' Then the people of Nineveh believed in God" (Jonah 3:4-5).

Some of you are thinking there must be more to the story. You may have had evangelistic campaigns, revival meetings, house-to-house canvassing, or a host of other evangelism programs in your church without seeing such results. And indeed, there is more to the story of Jonah. I remember listening to Vance Havner expound on Jonah's success. He said, "The people of Nineveh believed Jonah's message because when they looked into this prophet's face, they saw the eyes of a man who had just come back from the dead." Jonah wasn't the same man who had earlier refused to obey God. He had been to the depths and tasted the horror of death. When the great fish vomited him up on dry ground, Jonah knew what it meant to be delivered from death. The people of Nineveh saw this and believed.

Rekindling a Spiritual Fire in Our Hearts

Can any of us sincerely believe we are spiritually equipped to draw sinners into an eternal relationship with the living God just because we have completed a course in personal evangelism training? Is the secret to soul-winning found in the methodology we have mastered? Are we guaranteed a significant evangelistic harvest because we have outgoing personalities or have acquired many friends? We betray our spiritual poverty by even imagining such foolishness.

Recently, Dick Krenz, pastor of Immanuel Baptist Church in Wausau, Wisconsin, spoke at our church's twenty-fifth anniversary service and said, "God intends that our lives be just as supernatural as the crucifixion and resurrection of the Lord Jesus Christ." He was really asking the twentieth-century Jonahs to stand up and be counted.

Effective evangelists must do more than communicate secondhand information. Christian witnesses can only succeed if they are eyewitnesses of what the living Christ is doing. Our power in sharing the Gospel comes from living out Christ's death and resurrection. Do you count your old life to have terminated at the cross? Are you captivated by the thought that Jesus Christ is living in you? This is where the power for evangelism comes from.

In *The Pursuit of God*, A.W. Tozer suggests that the difference between the scribes of Jesus' day and the prophets of any age is that scribes talk about what they have read, while prophets talk about what they have seen. No wonder the angel told Zechariah, "'Not by might nor by power, but by My Spirit,' says the Lord" (Zech. 4:6).

Anything God wants done can be counterfeited by human energy and creativity. When we leave God out of the picture, though, the results of our efforts do not last. Richard Owen Roberts in his book *Revival* (Tyndale) gives us a taste of fleshly evangelism.

> Personal witnessing can be, indeed often is, nothing more than dead work. It is possible to witness to another without any feelings of compassion, without any deep concern for the lostness of the person witnessed to, and without significant reliance upon the Holy Spirit. Some appear to witness more for the purpose of adding up converts than for the glory of God. Others witness more out of compulsion than compassion, more out of habit than heart-felt interest in the lost and dying. (pp. 89–90)

Years ago, James Brand penned his own anguish over the flippant and superficial evangelistic strategies that were being busily carried on around him.

> There seems to have been for the last few years an undue exalting of the human element in revivals, instead of laying hold directly of God Himself. . . . People have been looking too much to externals, to methods, to men, to machinery, to "some new things," and not enough to self-abasing, heartbroken, holy prayer. ("Sermons from a College Pulpit," p. 43, as quoted by Roberts in *Revival*, p. 91)

I just read about a young lady who camped out all night in front of a Ticketron outlet in order to purchase tickets for a Bruce Springsteen concert the next day. Failing in the attempt, she ended up paying $300 to a ticket scalper. Now that is what I call devotion! I have never seen a Christian camp out in front of the church on Saturday night to be in a better position to hear the preacher the next morning. I have never seen a believer pay $300 to reserve a seat at a prayer meeting.

Perhaps this says something about why we are failing. George Verwer, director of Operation Mobilization, says that all the men, methods, money, and machinery won't succeed in fulfilling the church's evangelistic mandate until individual Christians are broken of the self life and in its place enthrone Jesus Christ as Lord of everything. Our success depends on being consumed by Christ.

Maybe it would be appropriate for you to go to some quiet place and take stock of your life by asking some hard questions. Do I spend more time watching television than engaging in spiritual pursuits? Do I love to make more money so that I can buy expensive things? Do I have a superficial prayer life? Have I ever led anyone to Christ? Have I ever really tried to lead a friend to Christ? Do I look for excuses to avoid going to church? Do I find myself daydreaming when I open my Bible? Are there secret sin patterns in my life that I enjoy encouraging? When was the last time that I spent an hour in prayer? When was the last time I cried for the sheer joy of knowing Christ's love? Am I critical of my pastor's sermon delivery? Do I resent having to tithe? Can I watch television violence and perversion and be fascinated rather than disgusted? Does the quality of my Christian life change with the company I keep? As you ask these questions, you may conclude that you have lost your first love—the fire has grown cold. Why not determine to rekindle the fire?

The Fire of Revival

It would be easy for me to fall into a popular trap by trivializing spiritual revival and reducing it to a series of religious formulas and cliches. I cringe when I hear a pastor say, "We are going to have a revival at our church next Sunday!" It is not that easy. In spite of sincere attempts to know God better, many saints have found the pathway to be a constant struggle!

Because we are not God, we must necessarily limit ourselves to what history has shown us about the way in which God's people began to seek His face, open their hearts, and beg Him for a fresh manifestation of His glory and power. Richard Owen Roberts, who has devoted his life to the study of revivalism, suggests that whenever God has met His people in an extraordinary way, five factors have been present.

Extraordinary need. One of the men on our pastoral staff attended a prayer conference in Seoul, Korea. He was captivated by the leadership team of an extraordinary Korean church and returned to the United States convinced that he had witnessed a portion of Christ's church upon whom the Spirit was pouring out authentic revival. His first words at the next pastoral staff meeting were something like this: "They've got it straight in Korea! There, the order of things is prayer first, then revival, and then evangelism!"

Just then our youth pastor broke in, "If evangelism is precipitated by revival, and revival is precipitated by prayer, what precipitates prayer?"

There was a moment of deafening silence. Then one word was whispered, "Desperation." Are you desperate enough to seek God's face?

One of the secrets of holy living is recognizing that our fleshly nature is incurably corrupt. It never improves, but it can be overshadowed and outvoted. The Apostle Paul exhorts us to "make no provision for the flesh in regard to its lusts" (Rom. 13:14). Defeat after defeat after personal defeat can produce a sense of desperation. You realize that only by allowing the Holy Spirit to referee in your heart can you defeat the impulses of the flesh. You desire this sincerely, but do you want it desperately? Are you willing to confess all known sin to God and by His power be done with it? Are you ready to give all the secret closets of your life to the Lord? Ask yourself one question: *What area of my life do I find hardest to yield to Christ?* Then yield it. Claim God's Word that sin shall not have dominion over you because you are under God's grace. Humble yourself before the Lord and tell Him how thirsty you are for spiritual reality. Read out loud Psalm 42:1-2, 4: "As the deer pants for the water brooks, so my soul pants for Thee, O God. My soul thirsts for God, for the living God. . . . I pour out my soul within me." Tell the Lord exactly how you feel.

Extraordinary awareness. Roberts says, "God can be expected to send revival when these extraordinary needs are extraordinarily felt" (p. 63). He continues, "If there is still something a person thinks he can do to save the day, he is unlikely to feel the need of an extraordinary measure." Are your spiritual nerve endings becoming highly sensitized? Are you starting to mourn about your evangelistic impotence? Are you aware that Christ is the answer, but frustrated because you are not telling anyone about Him? If so, the Spirit is working.

Extraordinary sense of God. Several years ago, my friend Steve's spiritual life was in shambles, but as much as he rebelled against God's will, he could not escape the Lord. Spiritual thoughts consumed Steve. He knew that God was giving Him another opportunity to straighten out his life. Steve reminded me of King David, who wrote in Psalm 139: "Thou hast searched me and known me.... and art intimately acquainted with all my ways.... Thou hast enclosed me behind and before, and laid Thy hand upon me.... Where can I go from Thy Spirit?... When I awake, I am still with Thee.... Search me, O God, and know my heart; try me and know my anxious thoughts; and see if there be any hurtful way in me" (vv. 1, 3, 5, 7, 18, 23-24).

Extraordinary prayer. A pastor confided in me that he had come to a decisive point in his ministry. He felt he could not go on unless the Lord rekindled a fire in his heart. So desperate was he that he kissed his wife good-bye and went to a secluded motel room. He opened his Bible, put it on the bed, got down on his knees, and stayed that way for days. Hours were spent in contemplative prayer. This was no game. He knew that his ministry—his very future—was being decided in that room. God honored his prayer. God gave him what he needed—a fresh vision of the work God had for him to do.

Extraordinary glory. Richard Owen Roberts writes, "God can be expected to send revival only when there is a people prepared to give Him all the glory" (p. 69). This is a perfect time to ask yourself why you want to evangelize. Consider your motives, for it is easy to be misled here. We all know people who have been praised in their congregations because of their track record in evangelism. Such recognition can so easily be coveted. The proper motive for evangelism is found in the desire to obey the two supreme commandments of the Scriptures: Love God and love your neighbor. When we love God, life's greatest delight is bringing honor to Him by expanding His kingdom. When we love our neighbors, we want to see them delivered from their sins. We know that God triumphs in their deliverance, and both of these supreme commandments are honored.

The Revived Soul-winner

Through the years I have watched many people get excited about evangelism—for a short time. They take classes, learn answers, make a decision to participate, and are off ringing doorbells. Sometimes they are carried along for a while by a particular environment, but when the environment changes, so does their commitment to evangelism.

I have a friend, Nate, who would never describe himself as an evangelist. Yet he has won many international students to Christ through years of working with them at the University of Wisconsin. To me, he manifests the four life qualities that suit a person for sharing his faith effectively over the course of a lifetime.

Personal repentance—pursuing the lordship of Christ. What comes to mind when you think of repentance? Vows to quit smoking? Someone weeping and wailing? An emotional experience? We would do well to think of repentance not as an act so much as a process. Repentance is a continual process whereby we bring our thoughts and actions into alignment with God's will. Christ expressed the essence of repentance when He said, "If anyone wishes to come after Me, let him deny himself, and take up his cross, and follow Me" (Mark 8:34). Repentance is a change of mind that prompts you to change your direction so you can follow Christ more closely. Depraved people are determined to live their own way; they do not want to hear about God's claim on their lives. When we repent, we come to our senses and want more than anything to do the will of Christ, our rightful Owner, who bought us with His blood. Think of repentance as a daily process—constantly realigning ourselves, exercising spiritual sensitivity, being open to whatever God asks us.

That is the outlook of the soul-winner.

Persistent prayer—depending on God's power. Just as repentance and lordship are two sides of the same coin, so are prayer and dependence. We start to pray for evangelistic opportunities when we begin to believe that God is at work preparing hearts. The more we see God's part in opening doors for evangelism, the more we will pray. It is inconceivable to me that one could separate evangelism from prayer. As we go about our business each day, we should be whispering, "Is this the one, Lord? Open doors, Lord; manifest Your power!" And that is only the beginning of how prayer relates to evangelism. Through prayer, we intercede for those who burden us. My friend Nate sometimes says, "Dick, it has finally happened. Ahmad has put his trust in Christ. I have been praying for him for two years."

Genuine concern—caring for people. Nate tells me that Americans who only talk about Christ do not leave much of an impression on international students. But when a Christian cheerfully meets an international student's need—when genuine concern is manifested—friendship and trust develop that will one day open the door for sharing.

Infinite patience—living by God's timetable. Many of us would profit from following Nate around for a week. He spends much time in the Word and in prayer. He takes time to strategize and think through objectives. When you are with him, you never get the idea that he is in a hurry to bring up the Gospel. He believes in "always being ready" as it says in 1 Peter 3:15. But to be ready to share, he must be ready to drive to the airport, to run an errand at the grocery store, or to invite a student into his home. Only when we are ready for these interruptions (and think of them as opportunities) will we be ready to share Christ.

Will you take time to pray about these four qualities? Are they present in your life? What can you do to make room for them? Which one strikes you as being most needed in your life? Start rekindling the fire.

Rekindling a Fire in Our Churches

If I understand the purpose of the local church, it is to make the things of God visible on the earth. God is a spirit; no one has seen Him at any time. It is through the local church that the attributes of God become visible.

All churches reflect value systems, but what value system does our church reflect? Pastors and other overseers set the tone here. They must constantly evaluate the message their church communicates, be watchful for hidden agendas, and question whether their church is really reflecting their stated values.

Will you ask yourself some hard questions about your church?

1. Do we share a vision for why we exist?

2. Are our decisions about our role in our community based on fear or faith? Are we protecting tradition or truth?

3. Are we really a company of the committed, determined to help one another follow God and to complete His work on earth?

4. Do we have a genuinely supernatural orientation to life? Do we believe that God still works miracles?

5. Is living out God's truth more important to us than enjoying creature comforts? Are we convinced that heaven is really our home?

6. Do we sometimes lapse into a fortress mentality that insulates us from contact with the world?

7. Is it obvious that we sincerely enjoy and respect each other?

8. Do we share a conviction that there are truths worth dying for?

9. Are we ever content with the status quo?

10. Do we feel that our local church is better or more important than others?

11. Do our leaders' decisions signal that our church building is more important than people?

12. Are we really people of prayer who depend on God continuously?

13. Are we open to the Holy Spirit's leadership?

14. Are we committed to the proposition that Christ is the only way to God and apart from Him people are truly and eternally lost?

The first step toward rekindling evangelistic fires in our churches is honest evaluation of where we are. We may discover that we aren't where we thought we were. Not much can happen in local congregations until church leaders share a common vision, write a clear purpose statement, and educate their people from the Scriptures concerning how they came to embrace this philosophy of ministry.

I urge you to consider a commitment to a *penetration philosophy* with the goal of permeating your community and your world with the knowledge of Christ. What a challenge! Here is a goal so vast that it will capture the imaginations of your most energetic and idealistic people. Here is a challenge so monumental that you know you will fail if you don't work together.

One of the great problems in our churches today is boredom. Do you sense that people are restless because they aren't being challenged to give themselves to an eternal cause that is worthy of every sacrifice they will ever make for it? We need to be challenged. Apart from a challenge, people easily fall into sin. Proverbs 29:18 says, "Where there is no vision, the people are unrestrained [or cast off their restraints]."

Because we tend to be so bound up in our traditions, our fears, and our comfortable ways, it is not easy to rekindle a fire in our churches. Let me offer a few suggestions about how churches can light revival fires again.

Selecting leaders according to biblical standards. Paul gave Timothy clear guidelines for selecting the primary overseeing team in the church (1 Tim. 3:1-7). Place in nomination only those men who have shepherd hearts, who have demonstrated a capacity to reproduce their spiritual lives in others, and who have open minds and a belief in the worldwide ministry of the church.

Do not place in nomination people who are merely nice or good in business, or who make it clear that they will be upset if they are not nominated. Do not place in nomination those who see the church primarily as a building or a business. Look for Spirit-filled leaders who believe in evangelism and who share their faith as a way of life.

So much depends on leadership. For the most part, if church leaders share a philosophy of ministry, so will the congregation; if church leaders are split right down the middle, the congregation will be also. It is not enough for potential candidates to be moral. They must share the vision of the church.

Pray together. You probably know a church where the prayer time on prayer meeting night is five minutes long. What does that say about our sense of dependence on God?

So many wonderful things happen when a congregation starts to take prayer seriously! Be creative in the way you pray. Break up into small groups and pray for every continent; come back together and pray for your community outreach; pair off and pray for individual needs; come back together and praise the Lord. Always pray by name for persons who need the Lord. Pray for conversions each Sunday that result from the hearing of the Word. Listen carefully to every request shared. In this way, you will learn how essential prayer is.

Prayer ought to be a vital part of Sunday worship. Pray for crisis situations around the world. Pray for missionaries every time they go back to the field. Pray for what God is doing through other churches in your community. Pray that God will call your young people into ministries all over the world. Pray that every member of the fellowship will have an evangelistic encounter during the upcoming week.

You may also want to set aside evenings of prayer or even whole nights of prayer. People who participate in such gatherings always comment on how wonderful it is to share requests, to sing, and to pray in an atmosphere free of time constraints. Such nights form unforgettable memories in the minds of God's people.

Hunger for revival. When revival is truly desired, church leaders will begin to take seriously their responsibility to deal with sin in the church. Often, the little foxes of sin subtly nip away at relationships in the church. Bitter people can destroy completely the winsome fragrance of Christ in the body. When was the last time church leaders cared enough about the glory of God and His reputation in the world to go to a crusty saint and admonish him about his negative attitude?

Revival depends on more than just dealing with obvious sin. It hinges on a fundamental openness to God's will. It is precisely this quality of openness to the "new thing" God wants to do through us that is lacking in many of our churches today. Closed attitudes only quench the Spirit.

Integrate concern for a world of lost people into every aspect of the church's ministry. World evangelism must not be the theme of mission conferences alone. It must be one of the great melodies that is constantly woven throughout the entire symphony of the life of the church. Let music, pastoral prayer, special greetings, and women's, men's, and youth ministries all relate to the big picture of the church. How does each one contribute to fulfilling the Great Commission?

If you are concerned about significant evangelism, get down on your knees and start praying for your church. Pray that the Holy Spirit will rekindle a fire there. But be careful not to become a superspiritual critic yourself. Be an enthusiastic and encouraging force in your church; refuse to get discouraged; and always keep before your eyes the big picture of what God designed His church to accomplish.

Rekindling a Fire in Our Communities

In *Revival*, Richard Roberts shares a thrilling vision of what will happen when the Spirit of God breaks loose on an entire community.

> Can you imagine the entire Body of Christ moving throughout the earth with unified purpose and Holy Spirit power? If that concept is too vast for your mind, think in terms of your own community. Consider every church member marching together in perfect harmony—every individual sharing precisely with every other individual the heartbeat of Jesus Christ. Imagine not one sleeping Christian left, not one backslidden believer remaining, but all alike devout and intent on seeing the will of Jesus Christ accomplished. To this startling picture add the same power of the Holy Spirit that transformed bumbling Peter into a Pentecost preacher. Unleash all this transforming power against the forces of sin and evil in your community. That is what revival is. (p. 20)

If you are burdened about evangelism, reflect on this proposition: The work of evangelism will not be accomplished by individuals alone, but rather by whole communities of believers who, through united prayer, have been cleansed, transformed, and energized by the Spirit of God.

How is this possible? How can Christians with centuries of historic differences unite together? Before speaking to that question, let's examine the obstacles that have prevented the saints from working together. Of course, there are the organizational labels: Baptists feel uneasy working with Presbyterians. Add to this closed theological systems: Dispensationalists don't trust those who embrace covenant theology. Then there are differences in church governance and liturgy. A great obstacle has been the holiness controversy. How do "twice-blessed" saints fellowship with those who do not accept the theology of a second work of grace? Still another stumbling block through the centuries has been the baptism controversy. It is no wonder that saints have found it difficult to cooperate with each other in fulfilling the Great Commission.

One possibility for unity remains (and it is not formal ecumenism in which the unity of the Spirit is confused with organizational union). I believe Christians can cooperate enthusiastically only when they share the conclusion that there are only a few cardinal truths that form the core of the Christian faith. These are the truths worth dying for. These are the truths that can unite Christ's church in cooperative activities.

What are these truths? I am not a theologian, but such a body of cardinal truths would probably include these ten points.

1. There is but one God in heaven, existing as three coeternal Persons—Father, Son, and Holy Spirit—to whom every human being is accountable.
2. The Bible is God's accurate and complete revelation of His changeless truth for humanity.
3. Jesus Christ, God's unique Son, is both fully God and truly man.
4. The Bible accurately declares that Jesus Christ was virgin born, sinless, offered on the cross for our sins, raised bodily from the dead, and will one day come again to earth.
5. Man is naturally sinful, separated from God, and completely

unable to save himself.

6. Our deliverance was made possible through the saving work of Christ's crucifixion (He died as our sin bearer) and resurrection.

7. We are justified through faith in Jesus Christ alone, at a point in time, and therefore can know the genuine assurance of sins forgiven and the reality of new life in Christ.

8. Christians are totally dependent on the power of the Holy Spirit, who indwells every believer, for victory over sin in their daily lives.

9. The visible church on earth ought to reflect the nature of the invisible church of all times and places and commit itself to fulfilling the Great Commission.

10. Those who trust Christ as Saviour and Lord will spend eternity in heaven; those who reject Him will spend eternity in hell.

Based on such a statement, cooperation could be possible among people who span the spectrum on the baptism issue, the holiness issue, the governance issue, the liturgical issue, and the issue of organizational or denominational affiliations. May the God of heaven ignite a Holy Spirit fire under the saints of every community, compelling them to work cooperatively in reaching their communities with the Good News of Christ!

Thinking It Over

● What happens when evangelism is performed merely in the power of the flesh?

● What is the relationship of revival to evangelism?

● What is the relationship of prayer to successful evangelism?

● What is the relationship between repentance and the lordship of Christ?

● Do you feel the stirrings of revival in your church? in your community?

CHAPTER 12
WORSHIP IN THE EVANGELISM PROCESS

If therefore the whole church should assemble together ... and an unbeliever or an ungifted man enters, he is convicted by all, he is called to account by all; the secrets of his heart are disclosed; and so he will fall on his face and worship God, declaring that God is certainly among you. (1 Corinthians 14:23-25)

Paul and Silas were worshiping God. The subject of their thoughts was how wonderful their great God was. All of this might seem rather normal except for the setting—they were in a Philippian jail cell in the middle of the night. They sat alone in the dark abyss of the inner prison singing hymns and praying. Their backs were still bleeding from the cruel beating they had received that day, yet they were worshiping—and the other prisoners were listening.

Luke tells us that in the midst of their worship there was a mighty earthquake that shook the very foundations of the prison and all the doors were instantly opened (Acts 16:26). The jailer was shocked out of his slumber and seeing the open doors, drew his sword to kill himself. Suddenly, he heard Paul cry out, "Do yourself no harm, for we are all here!" (Acts 16:28) The jailer was dumbfounded. Why hadn't the prisoners escaped?

I would like to believe that the prisoners stayed in jail because they wanted to hear the end of Paul's song! They were listening to true spiritual worship for the first time. I feel sure they were thinking something like this: "If these two men offer sincere and heartfelt worship to God after what they have just been through, their God must be truly wonderful."

That was almost two thousand years ago. Do such things happen today? Are people still captivated by authentic worship? Several months ago, I had lunch with Gordon MacDonald, who shared an exciting story from his former pastorate at Grace Chapel in Lexington, Massachusetts of how his friend had come to put his trust in Christ.

> My friend invited me out for lunch. As we were eating, he suddenly said to me in an enthusiastic voice, "I have just four questions for you today. How can I put my trust in Christ? Can I do it with you? Can I do it here? Can I do it now?" I don't think I can ever remember an evangelistic opportunity that was quite so ready-made! He had been coming to our services for several months and the Holy Spirit had obviously prepared his heart.

Worship: An Evangelistic Opportunity

When Gordon shared this story with me, my fascination was not so much with his witnessing experience as with what kind of atmosphere was present in his church that drew his unsaved friend there week after week. Grace Chapel has a wonderful reputation for providing a rich worship experience. When people from our congregation go to the East Coast, they love to visit Grace Chapel for the freshness of the worship experience there. God moves among His people.

Christians worshiping in spirit and truth constitute a significant and legitimate manifestation of God's glory to non-Christians who are present. Worship can be an evangelistic medium if it is conducted in joy and holiness that enable God to be seen through the worshiping community.

Francis Schaeffer, in his final book *The Great Evangelical Disaster,* reminds us that we live in a post-Christian era. We are naive to expect that unbelievers have any idea at all about what happens when Christians unite in worship. Could it be that by experiencing authentic worship non-Christians will be more likely to take the claims of Christ seriously?

Study the Book of Acts and you will discover that most of the converts heard the Gospel in a corporate way. Those who put their trust in Christ had the opportunity to see how Christians worship God and care for each other through a convincing demonstration. They were persuaded of the reality of Christianity by something they actually witnessed.

Let's consider how our worship experiences, both in church buildings and in other environments, might contribute to helping us fulfill our evangelistic mandate.

Worship True and False

Worship is the celebration of God's worthiness to rule over our lives and over His universe. We worship God by ascribing glory to His name through cultural expressions. We obviously choose the cultural forms with which we are most comfortable and which we consider to be respectfully appropriate.

God intends corporate worship to be an extraordinary experience. Through spoken word and hymns of praise, drama and poetry, prayer and psalter, we are to make His praise glorious. The very room in which we worship must announce His Presence: "God is among His people!" This is not a place where people are looking at their watches. "God is here!" hearts exclaim with joy and reverence. The living God is among us! His love overwhelms us! His very presence takes our breath away.

Our congregation is still learning about worship. Although we come from many different religious traditions, we sometimes catch a glimpse of authentic worship and are shocked by the power of the experience. On a recent Sunday, a man visiting our church said, "I've never been to a service like this. There is spiritual power in this room!"

As you try to get a handle on the meaning of worship, consider our Lord's conversation with the woman from Samaria (John 4). When He asked her for water, she was amazed that He would even talk to her; but He was opening the door to a spiritual conversation. Before long they were talking about water as a

symbol of the eternally satisfying experience of being in fellowship with God, and she sincerely asked for this living water.
Christ began to reveal her true heart problem to her. This set in
motion a series of questions, and the Lord's answers ushered her
into the life of the Spirit.

One of her first questions concerned the nature of God and
how He might be approached by people. She said to Jesus, "Our
fathers worshiped in this mountain, and you people say that in
Jerusalem is the place where men ought to worship" (John
4:20). To her, worship was far removed from everyday reality.

Christ answered her in a remarkable way: "An hour is coming,
and now is, when the true worshipers shall worship the Father
in spirit and truth" (John 4:23). Here, the Lord makes a distinction between true and false worship. True worship always has
two components. *Spirit* refers to the unifying relationship shared
by God and the worshiper. We can worship truly because we
have access to His presence, because we *know* Him! *Truth* is at
the very core of what we do when we worship. We praise God
for the true things we know about Him. Worship is not wishful
thinking! When God is met in spirit and truth, He is worshiped
in the beauty of holiness.

True worship is beautiful; false worship is repugnant. It is what
religious hypocrites do. This worship is based on human
thoughts and values, which are given a veneer of respectability
by ascribing them to God. But the inner spirit of man knows the
difference!

Spiritual worship centers on the idea of right relationship. We
worship God in spirit because we know Him and share His Spirit.
We are His. He is our Father. We love Him and are confident
that He loves us. Spiritual worship requires a right spirit within
us. It presupposes a clear conscience that frees us to be single-
minded. Spiritual worship also requires right relationships with
other worshipers. When relationships are right, worshipers feel a
freedom to respond to God creatively. Instead of trying to fit
into other people's expectations for proper worship, we sense
that our friends are giving us the liberty to worship God in
various ways.

Corporate worship is also beautiful because through it we can experience the thrill of sharing our common relationship with God. A member of my staff commented to me that as a child, an old-world type of liturgy completely turned him off. He felt a great hunger for meaningful relationships. Later he went to a church where people worshiped as if they knew God and loved one another. He was drawn to this place.

In contrast to our experience-oriented culture, we must worship God in truth. Biblical worship is not sentimentality or emotionalism. Worship is the response of heart, mind, and body to eternal truth about God. Worship loses its beauty if it is not based on the solid foundation of sound doctrine and the careful teaching of the Scriptures. Logically, the message about God should come first; then corporate expressions of praise that flow out of that message can be shared. We are trying to carry out this logical order in our church by having interactive evening services to allow worshipers to relate to the truth taught that morning.

True corporate worship, conducted in spirit and truth, is the most credible manifestation of the glory of God that I know of. Someone has wryly said, "The tragedy of our present world is that the charismatics worship God in spirit and the fundamentalists worship God in truth, but neither do both!" I don't think this is so, but if it were, neither group would be experiencing the beauty of true worship.

Attracting Non-Christians through Worship

The Willow Creek Church, pastored by Bill Hybels and located in Barrington, Illinois, is widely known for its evangelistic explosion of the last ten years. When this church began, it caused quite a stir. Some have accused Pastor Hybels of being too pragmatic. Others are uneasy about the church's nontraditional approach to worship. The success of this church has forced me to ask some tough questions.

Pragmatic worship. Can we be pragmatic in planning our worship services? This question requires some clarification. *Pragmatism* means "a system of philosophy that tests the validity of all concepts by their practical results." Such pragmatism is dangerous, because it denies absolutes. But isn't there a need for some pragmatic thinking? A pastor taking a pragmatic approach to worship might ask, "What are the issues people are talking about? What art forms do the people I want to reach identify with? What kind of music do these people listen to?"

I see the pragmatic approach as the opposite of the idealistic approach. The idealist is inclined to say, "There is one right way to do everything!" This includes worship. The pragmatist, on the other hand, believes there are a number of things that can make worship practical and relevant to people. Such a person is not afraid to try new things. The danger in the pragmatic approach is that by accepting the cultural forms, accommodations may be made for cultural values rather than upholding things eternal.

Every church, every pastor, ought to feel the excitement of presenting eternal truth in a relevant way. Both *forms* and *ideas* are promoted through culture. For example, in the United States today one popular idea espoused by our culture is that because nothing is absolute, nothing is wrong if it feels good. Contemporary music is one form for expressing this idea. The Christian pragmatist asks the question, "Can I communicate to my world through the *form* of contemporary music and still reject the *idea* expressed in so many contemporary songs?" Many think we evangelicals have been too afraid of such pragmatic approaches.

Timelessness worship. Our statements of faith declare that God is eternal. We know that Jesus Christ is the same yesterday, today, and forever. God's reality transcends any single cultural expression. But do we really express this idea in our worship? When I was a new Christian, I started attending a wonderful church. I loved the pastor, the preaching, the people, and the program. I was not familiar, however, with much of the music. It was music typical of another culture. It had once been a refreshing and meaningful context for communicating the excitement of Christianity, but its form was becoming irrelevant to many young believers.

Have we absolutized the forms of worship that were popular a century ago? Where is it written that worship services should last an hour? Where is it written that the pastoral prayer ought to follow the announcements and offering? Where is it written that the sermon must be preceded by a special musical selection?

Consider this Scripture: "If an unbeliever or someone who does not understand comes in while everybody is prophesying, he will be convinced by all that he is a sinner and will be judged by all, and the secrets of his heart will be laid bare. So he will fall down and worship God, exclaiming, 'God is really among you!'" (1 Cor. 14:24-25, NIV) Don't you long to have people from your community walk through the doors of your church, behold the beauty of worship that is conducted in spirit and in truth, and conclude that God is really among you?

God-centered worship. Now we must turn the coin over. Having talked about pragmatism and relevance, consider with me now God's holiness, His glory, His transcendence. People want to be introduced to a great God who is more than two inches taller than they. I hope you often feel like taking off your shoes when you enter into worship. I hope you experience the awesomeness of the Lord. This will be the case if your worship is God-centered. Our worship forms may change, but the object of our worship remains eternally the same.

In recent years as I have prayerfully considered the meaning of worship, I have found myself asking, Does every moment of our worship experience present a God-centered view of life? Do all of our worship activities help people see Jesus?

People want more than relevance—much more. Follow the people of your congregation through their weekly routine. Feel for them as they suffer disappointments and setbacks at their place of business. Many feel polluted by being exposed to almost constant profanity. Some come to church feeling desperate, wanting to be lifted above the grind of a confining, futile world. Most want to experience the power of the Scripture that says, "Cease striving and know that I am God" (Ps. 46:10).

With this in mind, we must ask hard questions. Do worship leaders and preachers perform for personal acclaim or are they windows through whom Christ can be seen? Do musicians communicate that God is great or that they are talented? Does the preaching of the Word hold a prominent place in your worship? Is Jesus Christ glorified as the answer to the great longings of mankind? A man-centered view of life takes us nowhere, but saints gathering together who evidence joy in celebrating God's worthiness can have an evangelistic impact on our communities.

Fresh worship. I have never met Anne Ortlund in person, but I admire her! My view of worship has been influenced by reading her masterful little book, *Up with Worship.* In a series of short but provocative chapters, she makes this point: There is nothing boring about the God whose name is Jehovah. You know this, but does your worship service affirm it in creative ways?

Is it possible that some of our traditionalism in worship formats is the consequence of lazy minds rather than spiritual conviction? In commenting on the need for vitality in worship, Stuart Briscoe quipped that stagnant churches share an unspoken motto: "As it was in the beginning, it is now and ever shall be!"

The answers given to life's toughest questions by secularists are leaving many people disillusioned. Politicians certainly don't have the answers. The glittering Hollywood scene appears to offer a way out, but its offerings quickly turn into familiar reruns. People are asking, "Where can I go to find a meaningful life? Who will explain to me what it means to live with significance? What does fulfillment look like?"

Let entire communities of believers respond with a manifestation of the power and glory of God. May our worship services announce to a disheartened society that God is alive and that life can be purposeful. Let the skeptic come to our worship services and leave having concluded that God is really among us!

A postscript must be written to this chapter. Although worship experiences are a legitimate evangelistic tool, we must not expect the pastor to be the evangelist. Bringing non-Christians to church is only one link in the chain that leads to conversion. Much of the rest is up to us as members of the congregation.

We manifest the reality of Christianity through corporate worship, but that is only one way. Spiritual reality can be seen in accepting people of diverse ideas, races, and economic strata. It can be seen in the way we relate to people with whom we disagree. It can be seen through the sacrifices we make as we try to serve one another. And there are many other ways.

Thinking It Over
● What would make a visitor keep coming to your church?

- Is *pragmatism* a dirty word when planning worship services? Is your church pragmatic in reaching out to your community?
- Is your church God-centered in worship?
- What would it take to produce the kind of spiritual environment that would attract non-Christians to your worship services?

CHAPTER 13
NEIGHBORHOOD PENETRATION AND EVANGELISM

Now all the tax-gatherers and the sinners were coming near Him to listen to Him. And both the Pharisees and the scribes began to grumble, saying, "This man receives sinners and eats with them." (Luke 15:1-2)

Do you really want to be like Jesus? Do you want to be a twentieth-century extension of His life and ministry? Does the idea of walking in His steps interest you? If we had walked the Galilean hills with Him, we might have discovered that He didn't spend all His time in the kinds of religious places many of us frequent.

Where would we have been most likely to find the Lord Jesus? He was usually with the people of the community. Luke offers us a striking picture of Christ's priorities for personal ministry.

Christ's Philosophy of Penetration
The first eleven verses of Luke 6 show that Christ had become a popular and controversial figure in Galilee. People had differing views about Him because He was healing on the Sabbath, and some believed this was contrary to the teachings of Moses. Luke tells us that the Master withdrew to a mountain and spent a night in prayer. After pouring out His soul to His Father for an entire night, He began the next day by selecting twelve men

with whom He could share and ultimately entrust His cause.

Immediately after calling the disciples, He took them down from the mountain to a great plain where they were engulfed by a great multitude of restless people. Luke tells us, "All the multitude were trying to touch Him, for power was coming from Him and healing them all" (6:19). What a dynamic moment! People were everywhere; there was noise, dust, pain, commotion. "And turning His gaze on His disciples, He began to say, 'Blessed are you who are poor'" (6:20). The verses that follow are pivotal for those of us who would be followers of Christ and who are committed to the ministry of evangelism. Jesus tells His disciples about the person who is blessed, the person who weeps, mourns, hungers, and so on. Then He contrasts these characteristics with what makes a human life pitiful. Woe to the person who is full and content! Do you see the picture? Jesus is engulfed in ministry, but His disciples are standing together apart from the crowd. Christ looks at them with compassionate eyes and says in effect, "Men, do you see where I am? Do you understand what your life will be like if you follow Me? I reject the status quo of this planet. If you follow Me, you must reject it too. Blessed are you if you are hungry and thirsty and hurting and irritated by what you see around you. Woe to you if you are content and satisfied to live in a world where people are lost and dying without trying to help them."

Do you really want to be like Jesus? Then go where people are, listen to their heart cries, and minister Christ's love to them at the point of their need.

When Jesus was about to die, He took His disciples to an upper room, instructed them, and prayed for them. He prayed that they would share His peace, but He also prayed that they would share His perspective.

I have given them Thy word; and the world has hated them, because they are not of the world, even as I am not of the world. I do not ask Thee to take them out of the world, but to keep them from the evil one. They are not of the world, even as I am not of the world. Sanctify them in the truth; Thy word is truth. As Thou didst send Me into the world, I also have sent them into the world. (John 17:14-18)

Christ reminds us that we must speak the truth in love to the world around us. Somehow Christians have to start talking to people other than Christians. In an insightful metaphor Jesus Christ calls us salt (Matt. 5:13). Just as salt is a preservative so we are to act to preserve His truth in the world. How pathetic when salt has no saltiness! This metaphor depicts a church that has no eternal message to share with the lost.

There are many other churches, however, who hold to eternal truth but whose people have no influence on their societies and speak only to themselves. They declare that their mission is to guard the truth, but because they are not reaching beyond their own walls, they do not know what to do with the truth. Instead of the lighthouse shining brightly on the shore, the light burns meaninglessly in an obscure basement.

Christ's plan is for the salt to come into contact with the world and still remain salty. If the salt of eternal truth is to permeate our society, we must develop a philosophy of penetration. Our model is Christ Himself: "Now all the tax-gatherers and the sinners were coming near Him to listen to Him. And both the Pharisees and the scribes began to grumble, saying, 'This man receives sinners and eats with them'" (Luke 15:1-2).

As we come to the concluding pages of this book, consider with me what our churches must become if they really want to penetrate their communities.

Rethinking Separation

The starting point for many of us is to rethink the biblical meaning of separation. Joe Aldrich in his book, *Life-Style Evangelism*, believes that few things have hindered the evangelistic success of the modern church so much as a faulty view of separation. Much of what is necessary to establish relationships with people would be viewed by some as a lowering of standards, which compromises our purity and leaves us contaminated.

What does separation really involve? Let's look at the life of Christ for a clue. The author of Hebrews tells us that Jesus Christ, as our perfect High Priest, was "holy, innocent, undefiled, separated from sinners and exalted above the heavens" (7:26). Now, turn to Matthew and you will find another picture of Christ: "The Son of Man came eating and drinking, and they say, 'Behold, a gluttonous man and a drunkard, a friend of tax-gatherers and sinners!'" (11:19) He was separate from sinners, yet a friend of sinners! Obviously, separation was not understood by the Saviour in terms of what He ate or drank. Separation meant that Christ's heart was given entirely to the Father. His heart was broken by the sinfulness of people around Him, but He continued to love and spend time with them.

Sometimes my children ask, "Dad, is it OK to have non-Christian friends?" My answer to them is that it all depends on why. Do you want such friendships because you are really infatuated by a worldly lifestyle? Do you want to be with them because you envy their "anything goes" worldview? Or do you want to be with them because you care for them and want them to know your Saviour?

I don't think it is possible to overstate how important it is for all of us to rethink this matter of separation. A philosophy of community penetration dictates that we be mature enough to discern between biblical separation and spiritual isolationism. Jesus Christ is calling upon us to share His vision: separated from sin, friend of sinners. Are we really open to what God wants to do?

Committing the Church to Neighborhoods and Community Organizations

Our church attracts worshipers from many places in the surrounding area, some from distances of more than twenty-five miles. As we recognize this fact, some of us wonder if there isn't a convenient way to bring the Good News of Christ into a hundred neighborhoods. We have a man on our staff who lives to see this dream realized. Jim Tanner is quietly working to make sure that every neighborhood in Madison has an evangelistic witness. Let him speak for himself:

In keeping with the conviction that evangelism is most successful in the context of natural affinities and that closely boundaried neighborhoods can provide an affinity base, we have established neighborhood groups in as many neighborhoods as available, qualified leadership allow.

Each neighborhood group meets twice a month at the time of their own choosing. Each biweekly session consists of five components: fellowship, sharing (both personal victories and prayer requests), prayer, the study and application of the pastor's Sunday morning sermons, and some consideration of how to reach out evangelistically to neighbors. Currently, we have about 125 people participating in these groups. Our goal is to establish viable cells in at least twelve other neighborhoods before the end of the year.

I am encouraged by the things that are happening in the lives of our neighborhood group members, but we are only scratching the surface.

How are you strategizing to bring the ministry of your church into various neighborhoods of your community? A philosophy of penetration demands such thinking.

When I pastored the Aurora Free Church in Aurora, Nebraska, one of our members was kind enough to invite me to join the local Rotary Club. Being a big city boy, I had no idea of how strategic that decision would be. Through my participation in that organization, I developed a personal relationship with almost every business and civic leader of our community. My present involvement with the Y.M.C.A., the Walnut Grove Home Association Board, and the Dane County Evangelical Pastors' Fellowship is not extraneous to my sense of mission; it is an essential component of penetrating my world.

Your church might consider establishing a special committee to identify and penetrate the social and civic organizations of your community. For this bold adventure to succeed, pastors must release busy people from daily participation in church activities so they have time for civic penetration.

Rethinking the Use of Our Facilities
Not too many years ago, our church was approached by a woman from outside our church who asked if her basketball team

could use our gym to train for a city league. Unfortunately, the church leaders were caught off guard. We found ourselves wrestling with the question of how our church facility relates to community affairs. Predictably, some raised the question of separation. "Won't our witness be diluted if non-Christians use the facility?"

Our trustees wisely began to ask a more appropriate question: "How can we have a ministry to non-Christian groups who use our facility?" This is the question that ought to be asked in churches throughout America.

Evangelistic Programs

Let me share a personal observation. Churches have opted out of evangelism simply because it is so costly. People don't usually become Christians without a struggle and without a lot of love, patience, and personal concern shown to them. In Luke's account of the Parable of the Sower, good seed produced good fruit on good soil, but "with perseverance" (8:15). Evangelism also needs perseverance.

Time is so valuable! We all want to use our time better because we know it is important to be good stewards of the twenty-four hours God entrusts to us each day. Since we are concerned about time, we tend to want to speed up the process of evangelism. It cannot be done. How then shall we allot time for evangelism?

Friendship ministries. Every local church ought to have a friendship ministry. Personable and outgoing people should be encouraged to set aside one night a month (it may be more frequent) to visit those who are new to the church. Oftentimes evangelistic opportunities will result. I am not sure this is the best approach, but every time I am ready to abandon it altogether the Lord brings to mind someone who came to Christ through such a visit.

Home Bible studies. Last week I received an unusual invitation. The young adult class at the church I previously pastored in Chicago invited me to a special class reunion. This young adult class was no ordinary Sunday School class. There was a special dynamic present that resulted in attendance of well over a hundred people each week.

The leadership of that class was composed of people who were won to Christ through two small home Bible studies. One of these studies, held in our home, resulted in more than a half dozen people receiving Christ as Saviour. The other study has seen hundreds come into the kingdom, and it continues to this day.

I believe history will record that in the last half of the twentieth century, more people were won to Christ through home Bible studies than through any other way. Such studies enable a person to hear the facts of Christianity over a period of time while watching Christians in action. They also enable a new believer to be discipled in a comfortable way.

These studies can be evangelistically fruitful if they focus on a specific theme for a given period of time. What would happen if a couple prepared fliers for everyone in their apartment complex announcing they were having an eight-week study of the Bible to discover secrets of a happy marriage? Another fruitful study might be entitled The Place of Religion in American Politics. Still another might be Everything You Always Wanted to Know about the Future but Were Afraid to Ask!

Special events. What kind of ministry would you assign a Big Ten football coach who attended your church? The late Coach Dave McClain loved the Lord and was not ashamed to testify to this in public. Knowing this, we held several evangelistic breakfasts for men. Once or twice a year, fathers and sons met together on Saturday morning for these special events. We invited members of the University of Wisconsin football team and showed football movies; then people like Dave McClain shared how they came to know Christ.

The women of our church have a special women's banquet each year as well. Scores of guests come to special events like these.

Are you planning special events in your church with evangelism in mind? This may be a function of your church's outreach committee, but evangelistic strategizing ought to be built into the purpose of every organization and committee in the church. Such strategizing is healthy and enriching.

A Time for Commitment

As you near the end of this book, it is time for you to make an important commitment. I hope you have learned a lot of fresh material about the Gospel of Christ. What will you do with it? You may even have come to know Christ through this encounter. If you have, I would love to hear from you so that I can share your joy. Most of you, however, are "establishment Christians." You know you are no Billy Graham, but you are honestly concerned that over 3 billion people in the world need to hear the Good News about Jesus Christ.

Before you let the appalling number of needy people immobilize you, remember something: an evangelistic explosion has already shaken the foundations of the planet earth. It happened once. It can happen again.

This brings us back full circle to our basic thesis. We have asked one central question: What will it take to produce an evangelistic explosion in the twentieth century? Prayerfully consider my conclusions.

First, it will take a memory. I hope you will never allow yourself to get too far away from the Book of Acts. Dr. Luke reminds us that our God is powerful and vitally involved in His creation. What happened in Jerusalem, Antioch, and Ephesus in the early church was extraordinary. Incredible forces of darkness held sway over our planet when Jesus Christ was born, but all the hosts of hell could not prevent the light of Christ from penetrating the first-century world by the power of the Holy Spirit. If you really take time to consider what happened then, you will abandon your pessimism about the present. A negative attitude will give way to prayer, planning, and anticipation.

A contemporary evangelism explosion will also require a message—*the* message. There is only one Gospel: Christ died for our sins and rose victorious from the grave. Saving faith means personally making a choice to depend on Christ's finished work. The cross is God's doorway to deliverance from sin and its consequences. If your heart responds to this message, you will abhor the notion of trying to bring people into the kingdom through an emotional experience, a sacrament of the church, or a superficial change in lifestyle. You will compassionately point out to people that they are lost in their sins and need to break through the "guilt barrier" by admitting their spiritual need, and you will point them to Christ crucified, for He alone is our hope.

What will it take? A fresh methodology, for we need a clear way to present the Gospel to others. I hope you have profited by our study of the four crucial issues.

Finally, prayerfully confess that there will be no twentieth-century explosion apart from a manifestation of the power of God among us by His Holy Spirit: "For from Him and through Him and to Him are all things" (Rom. 11:36). The bottom line in evangelism is that we do not save people. We are only heralds of truth. Occasionally God has been pleased to bring revivals to His church during which thousands of people have been won to Christ. I am convinced that we will never see significant evangelism again apart from revival in the church and extraordinary prayer.

Are you really interested in evangelism? Then consider what it means to be holy and prayerful and single-minded. The call to evangelism is really the same as the call to follow Christ. The master Evangelist said:

A pupil is not above his teacher; but everyone, after he has been fully trained, will be like his teacher. (Luke 6:40)

Follow Me, and I will make you fishers of men. (Matt. 4:19)